Lies and Truth

Lies and Truth

Marcel Eck

TRANSLATED BY

Bernard Murchland

The Macmillan Company, New York, New York
Collier-Macmillan Limited, London

Contents

Introduction

IT IS NOT OUR intention to write a treatise on morality in which all aspects of the problem of lying will be finally resolved.

The moral aspect of lying will scarcely be touched upon. We shall insist much more upon psychological conditions, both normal and pathological.

We shall make every effort to avoid undue emphasis upon the negative aspects of lying and bad faith in order to develop the positive consequences of our research. In other words, we will stress everything that may be considered the opposite of lying: loyalty, sincerity, and fidelity. We also shall have occasion to touch upon particular aspects of witness, confession, and certain situations related to professional life where the obligation of secrecy can occasion problems of conscience with respect to the truth.

The problem of truth will be our main concern, for it is not so much a question of hating lies as discovering and loving the truth. That is why this study begins and ends with two studies on truth. The first will investigate the discovery of truth by the child; the second will attempt to show that the passion for the living truth is the only true remedy against lying.

Too narrow a conception of truth and falsehood would risk being sterile. Consequently, we shall discuss the role of the imagination as it is manifested in myth and fiction.

We warn the educator not to expect a handbook of recipes on how to combat lying. Insofar as we succeed in showing that one must live in truth before offering principles to others will our objective be attained.

MARCEL ECK

Lies and Truth

I

The Discovery of Truth
and Negation

THE DISCOVERY OF TRUTH

WHO SAYS lie or bad faith refers, even though one may not be aware of it, to the notion of truth? There can be no falsehood except in relation to the truth or at least what we take to be the truth. We can form a false idea of the true, but in that case we are in error. To err and to lie are two different things.

We can study lying only after having tried to understand how a child acquires truth. Of course, it goes without saying that the pursuit of truth is a life-long occupation and at no time can we ever say that we possess the truth in its entirety. But that is another problem.

The child cannot be guilty of lying until he has become more or less consciously aware of the possibility of being a mediator between the true and the other and at the same time is aware of the possibility of concealing, deforming, or denying what he really knows.

This awareness is only gradually acquired and then never completely.

What is the *true* for a child? When we begin to investigate the problem of lying we shall see that truth is first of all that which is expected of him. Far from being an absolute, it is a relative mode of relationship to another.

The Self and the External World

A child acquires the notion of the true only after he emerges from his subjectivity into the objective world.

He must grasp the notion of a world external to himself that is constituted by *others*—objects that surround him and facts he can observe.

Falsehood is impossible until the notion of a world transcendent to oneself is recognized. What does child psychology teach us? The child comes to the notion of an external world only in a very gradual fashion. In the first weeks of his life he vaguely identifies with everything around him. The universe perceived by the eye is imprinted upon his retina and becomes one with it; the object he touches is merely the prolongation of his own hand. Melanie Klein holds that there is no initial differentiation between the child and his mother's body, which nourishes him. Despite the exaggeration this theory is prone to, there can be no doubt, before being an *object*, the mother is scarcely differentiated from the *subject*. Only by a gradual apprenticeship does the child become aware of his individuality with respect to the rest of the world. The mother becomes a beneficent object who appears or disappears according to the child's needs. Communication soon begins to take place: a smile is exchanged for a smile, the infant's crying commands the appearance of the desired maternal object. The plaything by the infant's side will gradually become distinct from his own organism. The external world he cannot reach with his hand will take on distance with respect to his retina.

Similarly, the child becomes aware of his *self*. Little by little he individualizes his bodily schema in terms of sensations, some of which are pleasant, others unpleasant. He thus succeeds in asserting himself as an individual and in taking his place in a world that is distinct from him, an external world that is animate or inanimate, itself a source of pleasant or unpleasant sensations, but a source that is differentiated from the self.

It is difficult to say exactly when the child becomes sufficiently aware of the world about him, of things and people, to realize, even in an incipient stage, the truth of his being and the truth of those things that are not him. The progressive character of this awareness does not permit us to fix an exact time. We are dealing here with a whole stage of development. Jacques Lacan has called it the mirror stage, which begins about the sixth month. At this age a child can identify with his image in the mirror; he recognizes and individualizes himself.

The beginning of this stage is rather blurred and varies with individual cases. But it is certain that the third party who puts the child before the mirror accelerates the recognition by insisting on the identity of the image and the person: "See the baby, that's a baby there," and hastens the advent of the mirror stage. We cannot say at what age a child would identify himself if he were left alone.[1] The educative intervention of the other is of capital importance. But this takes nothing away from the value of the fact itself. The idea of

[1] We know that female pigeons ovulate only in the presence of a partner. Yet ovulation does take place when they are put in a cage with a mirror. The pigeon perceives its own image as that of a different being.

the reality of the external world is at least as much the result of emotional and educational influences as it is of simple perception.

We cannot speak of falsehood until there is this awareness of the existence of a reality within oneself and external to oneself. Lying is defined with respect to the other, and, as we shall see, it must be distinguished from the absence of sincerity, which is a relationship with oneself. The absence of sincerity constitutes bad faith, which is a way of lying to oneself in order to better lie to others. Every lie is the recognition of a transcendence.

Lying and Language

Given the fact that lying is defined with respect to the other, is it possible to lie before acquiring the instrument of relationship and expression that is language? Everyone who has investigated the problem of lying has asked this question. Sutter, in his excellent book on childhood lying,[2] speaks at some length about this problem. We must point out that it is important to distinguish between children who use the third person and those who refer to themselves in the first person. There is essential difference in the relationship to reality between a child called James who says "James did that" and a child who says "I did that." The progression from "he" to "I" is an essential step. However, as E. Pichon emphasizes, it would be wrong to identify (as many do) the emergence of self-awareness with the use of the first-person pronoun. The use of the first person indicates an evolved rather than emergent sense of the self. There can be no doubt that the falsification of the truth precedes language. It begins with the sense of the forbidden, which the child acquires very early. It

[2] Sutter, *Le Mensonge*, Collection "Païdeia," P.U.F.

is not yet a question of lying in the full sense of the word, but the very young child is capable of deceptive behavior long before the development of language.

The very young child understands before he can express himself. He knows what is permitted and what is not and is thus capable of acting truthfully or deceptively.

But we must be careful not to assume the notion of responsibility when it does not yet exist. Pichon uses the word *illusion* and this is no doubt preferable to the term *lying* in the early stages of development because it does not imply the idea of guilt.

Here are two examples that show how the child's attitude toward the truth varies before the acquisition of language. M. does not yet talk. She notices that her mother places her ring on the edge of the sink when she washes her hands and does not always put it back on immediately. One day the ring disappears. M. was the only one in the bathroom. M. is shown a ring to make her understand what is lost. She then takes her mother's hand and leads her to a box of toys and points out the ring. She manifests an attitude of frankness because at bottom M. already knows that she is not allowed to play with her mother's ring.

Here is another example. R. does not talk. He was scolded several times for making crayon marks on the wall. One day R.'s father came into the room and saw strange white patches on the wall. The child had used wet paper to cover his crayon marks and thus revealed a naïve awareness of lying. R. could not talk but was already attempting to conceal something judged to be reprehensible.

Guy Durandin also denies that lying and language are necessarily related.[3] "In simulating suffering by his

[3] Guy Durandin, *Le Mensonge de l'enfant*, Annales médico-psychologiques, 1957, Vol. I, No. 2.

cries to obtain what he desires, the child has begun to lie before he knows how to talk." Cousinet cites the specific example of an eight-month-old child who emptied the contents of a dresser on the floor. His mother expressed displeasure and told the child to keep away. A few moments later he threw a toy under the dresser, thus fabricating a pretext to return to the dresser and its attractive contents. The term *pretext*, however, characterizes the child's deceitful conduct rather too consciously in light of the child's age; it would be more exact to say that the child simply created a situation that permitted him to return to the dresser.

This manner of lying seems to us very similar to what we were able to observe in a little girl who had already begun to talk. At the age of nineteen months she wanted to get up when her parents wanted her to stay in bed because it was cold. She waited for a few moments and then threw her doll on the floor, exclaiming: "I have to pick up my doll." In both cases the child created, by ruse or by words, a desirable situation.

Deceitful behavior appears, therefore, very early in the life of a child, at an age when there can be no question of a conscious act of lying. Lying at this stage is simply a means of realizing a desire.

We have all observed very young children playing games that are intended to deceive others. They have an awareness of what is forbidden long before they begin to talk and quickly assume deceitful attitudes in order to obtain a forbidden objective, although we certainly cannot speak of responsibility in such cases.

The advent of language perfects the possibility of expressing thought but at the same time increases the possibility of falsification. Aesop and his fable about language is not far off. I should here like to make a remark about the limits of language. This may seem superfluous in a chapter dealing with the discovery of truth, but it is nonetheless logical. The limits of language in the discovery of truth are marked by an encroaching ineffable, by a truth that is never attained and is still less expressible. This limitation represents more than a regressive factor. Language clarifies the truth but at the same time can never express the totality of the truth that we glimpse.

J.-M. Le Blond[4] has seen the possible confusion between truth that can be envisaged and truth that can be formulated. We beg the reader's indulgence for introducing Hegel into a chapter treating the discovery of the truth by children, but with Le Blond we can say: "Hegel insisted at length and with good reason on this point, emphasizing not only the difference but also the frequent opposition between the *gemeint* (what we want to say) and the *gesagt* (what we actually do say)." This, in our opinion, is an exact characterization of truth in process: It is always clearer when formulated, but the mold of words can never give adequate expression to it. Is there a transcendence of language that would permit of a better approach to the truth? Artistic expression is no doubt the only means of transcending language. Music is perhaps the most excellent of these aesthetic expressions. Some forms of abstract painting and music correspond to our need to express a felt truth that is not limited by the contingency of objectification. But, to return to our subject, can art lie? Can it deliberately deceive? To this I would answer: Yes. There is factitious art that exploits a desire to please and be fashionable. Such art is a falsification, even when it is sincere.

We seem to be far from the child's discovery and

4 J.-M. Le Blond, *Action populaire*, April 1958.

experience of the truth. And yet we are not. All child psychiatrists find more truth in a spontaneous drawing than in verbal expression. But this approach to a child's "truth" can be effective only on condition that we avoid interpreting such drawings in light of some *a priori* system, Freudian or otherwise.

It is clear that barriers, taboos, and interdictions have less place in the child's colors and drawings than in his verbal expression.

The True and the Imaginary

There can be no notion of the truth without an awareness of the independence of the self vis-à-vis the external world; no concept of lying without reference to this external world and others. Lying cannot be disassociated from the subject-object relationship or some form of intentionality. A lie is a work of intelligence undertaken for a specific end. But might not this relationship be falsified by a number of elements that denature the object or at least subjectivize it? It is certain that the play of the imagination can modify the notion of truth. While an adult usually distinguishes the real from the imaginary, the child rarely does.

The power of the imagination is considerable, particularly (as Sartre has pointed out) in distorting reality. The imaginary cuts us off from the real, but is it possible to conceive of any true consciousness without imagination? Is not an image also reality? We can no more conceive of a consciousness without imagination than one without the power to think, Sartre points out.

If we take a particularly uncontrolled form of the imaginary, such as dreams, we see a radical difference between the attitude of a child and that of an adult. While the adult may wonder whether he dreamed such and such or not, he can usually distinguish between dreaming and the waking state. He can do so because experience has taught him that dreams lack the logical structure of real-life events.

Even if we take into account the unreality of dreams and the hypnagogic images that precede them, it remains true that they betoken the power to imagine a subjective potential for warping the truth.

Neither adults nor children can exercise their imaginations except through the instrumentality of a subjective, personal construction, although we cannot speak of lying in this case. As Sartre remarks, the image is a form of consciousness, not a philosophy, and this consciousness is marked by the personality of each individual. With similarities of perception, the imagining consciousness of each marks the image with the seal of his individual personality.

Put ten painters before the Pont du Gard and you will have ten entirely different canvases, but we can still identify the celebrated Roman aqueduct in each one of them.

The child, much more than the adult, identifies truth with the image he has of it. He does not criticize the image but rather fuses it into a whole where it is impossible to distinguish what pertains to the domain of truth and what belongs to the imagination. We cannot accuse a child of lying who draws a glass house with transparent walls through which we see a table with a family gathered about it.

A child's truth transcends the truth of perception. The consciousness he has of the image of this or that thing is a syncretic, global consciousness in which the role of the imagination takes precedence over a critical notion of reality. Thus it is easy to see that the child's account of the truth can be contaminated by the imagination even though he has no intention of deceiving.

There is no question of error. This term is prescribed under the circumstances, for in reality what the child imagines or says is the projection not only of an image but also of an authentic emotional resonance. The image always implies an intentionality and, in the young child, this forms part of his incipient conception of the truth. It is intentionality that subjectivizes the child's thought and often deforms it although there is no desire to deceive. The intentionality of the image is altogether different from that of a lie.

Thus the child's truth is composed of a number of elements that fuse in a Gestalt:[5] Perception, emotional resonance, imaginary representation, and intentionality blend with what is feared and desired. This is evidently far removed from absolute truth. The child will often be much more at ease in pursuing an imaginary dream that satisfies what he desires rather than in confronting the real. This is one of the bases of the dialectic between the pleasure principle and the reality principle.

We do not imagine in a vacuum. We imagine on the basis of acquired experience, of what is known, and the image takes on intentionality in terms of a prior experience—which is to say that our education and perceptions play a role in the formation of the imagination. This will be important to recall when we come to discuss the essence of lying. For we always lie on the basis of acquired knowledge.

The child's imaginative projection plays a considerable role, and he discovers naturally his dominant images through the vague contours of what he observes. Julien Green tells us in the autobiography of his childhood that he really saw strange monsters in the

[5] Gestalt theory refers to an arrangement of separate units in a form, pattern, or configuration integrated so as to appear and function as a unit that is more than the simple summation of its parts.

curtain folds and floor designs of his room and they terrified him.

A child will see a flock of sheep in the clouds although he knows full well they are not sheep; the reflections in water will represent a whole phantasmagoric world fashioned out of what he already knows. By the power of his imagination, he projects a whole life into what surrounds him without being totally duped by it and without the least intention of deceiving, although it is quite possible that later he will in all good faith affirm that there was a flock of sheep in the sky or that the river was peopled with strange fish. The young child has not yet acquired the faculty of surprise; he imagines on the basis of what he knows but only later will he adopt a critical attitude toward his imaginary world.

Play is most frequently no more than an imaginary indulgence, and this can continue long after one's critical capacities have developed. This is often the case with adults who seek distraction in the imaginary long after they have ceased to believe in it.

Romain Rolland has given us an example of the child's powers of imagination. "He is in the house, sitting on the floor with his feet in his hands. He has just decided that the carpet is a boat and the floor is a river. He believes that he will drown if he leaves the carpet. He is surprised and somewhat disturbed when no one pays any attention to him. Finally, he catches his mother's skirt and says: 'Don't you see that this is water? You must take the bridge.'" Here is another example. One day R.'s mother found him in the corridor with his wooden truck. He was staring intently at a fixed point on the ceiling. "What are you doing there?" "Can't you see the light is red? I am waiting for it to turn before going on." R. did not lie in speaking about red and green lights. He knew very well that they did not exist. But he did not lie when he said he saw them. What he imagined and what he saw were one and the same truth for him. His behavior was motivated by the reality of the corridor and the imaginary signal lights; everything fused in his image of a corridor that had become a real street and a wooden truck that had become a real truck and an imaginary signal that had become real lights. Earlier, he had imagined that the doorknob was a gas pump. Later, he stopped suddenly because he imagined he had had a breakdown.

It would be a serious underestimation of the power of the imaginary to think that it is restricted to the domain of dreams or illusion. The imaginary involves genuine, real, and tangible reactions that testify to its dynamism. Satre notes that the merely imagined representation of light or darkness is sufficient to cause the dilation or retraction of the pupil. The imagining of a repugnant scene can cause nausea and an erotic scene can provoke somatic reactions whose voluptuous nature cannot be denied.

The Super-ego[6] and Prohibitions

We have seen how the child gradually becomes conscious of his individuality with reference to the external world and constructs an original "truth" on the basis of that world. This truth is modified by the imaginary, which in the child's young mind is confused with the real. The child's power of imagination perhaps warps the truth but at the same time gives it its dynamism by disclosing a certain intentionality that is the result of progressive experience and the natural tendency to satisfy, in the midst of and by means of the

[6] In Freudian language the "superego" is the largely unconscious element of the personality that dominates the conscious ego with a system of prohibitions that, if transgressed, cause feelings of guilt.

real, its instinctive tendencies. The dialectic of the imaginary and the real, the maturing contact with the reality principle that limits the pleasure principle, the clarification of perception and the image with the advent of language that concretizes the ego—all of this makes lying possible. But the essential fact is the consciousness of prohibitions and painful sanctions that conflict with the instincts, with the id.[7] Lying thus becomes a means of avoiding prohibitions and reprimand.

Perhaps falsified but also enriched by the imaginary, the truth will once again be called into question. But this time it will not be because of the inconsistency of dreams but because of unpleasant contact with powerful elders. The child will construct two truths: one that is his and satisfying; and another less gratifying truth which is that of his elders, primarily his parents. *True behavior* amounts to doing the will of adults. To lie is to go against what a mother or father wants. The criterion of respect for the truth will not be the absolute, which the child cannot yet attain or even envisage; it will be reward and punishment. To lie is to say something not expected by those in whom authority is vested. Lying and disobedience are often confused, since lying is voluntarily concealed disobedience.

The child will act as he is expected to without worrying about whether it is true or not; he will answer all questions in what seems to be the most agreeable fashion. He wishes to avoid a scolding and at the same time to please. This recalls the attitude of those Orientals who automatically give the most agreeable answers to questions put to them. One must be an Occidental to be fooled by this. A friend tells me that in the Near East he was often answered in this way. For example, while waiting for a bus he would ask the natives if it

[7] By the "id" Freud meant the world of the instincts.

was due soon. They often answered in the affirmative
because they took this to be the most pleasing response, although they had no intention to deceive. One
of my North African patients gave me some cause for
concern. I ordered her to take a month's rest, but she
refused. A more experienced doctor explained that I
didn't interpret her correctly. He told me that she
would take three days off, at the end of which time she
would announce a further delay and so forth until she
had fulfilled my original request. Not that she was
deceiving herself; it was just her way of doing things. I
learned, and it is difficult for an Occidental to do so, to
play along with her game.

It is often thus with children and primitive peoples
who have retained a childish spirit. Without any ill
intent a child might give a false answer because he
thinks it will please his parents, even though no sanction is threatened. One day the local pastor was unable
to hold his catechism class, so he let the children play
in the church. But Pierre told his parents that the class
took place as usual rather than admit he played with
the other children of the village, because he knew that
his parents wouldn't like that. Thus we see how on the
basis of the superego, on the basis of prohibitions and
taboos, a world of artificial truth is born to accommo-
date the concern for peace and respect for conformity.
We are here far from the level of morality! Sometimes
the child will even get caught in the contradiction of
lying in order to be believed. He confuses what is true
with what is most likely.

In this perspective, where there is not yet any question of responsibility, we can say that the discovery of
the possibility of lying is indicative of a certain degree
of intelligence. A person who lacks imagination or intelligence would be incapable of lying. From a psychological point of view, we could say that the discovery

of the possibility of lying marks the presence of an already evolved stage of the intelligence. This is not intended as an apology for lying, but we must recognize that the most intelligent are often the most deceptive and the most capable of lying. We have only to recall Ulysses. He was the best liar as well as the most intelligent of the heroes of the *Odyssey.*

Although the child is not aware of it and although we cannot initially impute guilt, the discovery of the possibility of lying (and in some cases the actual act of lying) is certainly evidence of the subject's individuality vis-à-vis the external world and his freedom to appropriate it imaginatively in terms of his pleasure or interests.

Lying is a freedom with respect to what is, and, for this reason, it cannot be reduced to other faults. But to speak of fault is already to situate ourselves on the level of moral responsibility. Let us point out, however, that lying is totally distinct from other faults, which are either the exaltation of self (pride, anger) or the exaltation of possessions (envy, avarice) or the exaltation of instincts (gluttony, lust, laziness). Lying is in a different category. It might abet other faults, but it can also be used for altogether different purposes. More than the others, it is an intellectual fault. It was by a lie that the serpent and sin entered the world. Lying is normally only a means, and when it becomes an end in itself it becomes pathological as in the case of depraved lying and mythomania.

Lying, Shame, and Fault

The stage in which lying is recognized as a true fault comes rather late and supposes an implicit notion of transcendent truth. Lying is the recognition of a transcendence. Lying among children can be considered truly culpable only when the age of reason dawns, which is to say around the seventh year. The age of reason corresponds to a psychological reality and is not merely an artificial indication of moral accountability. At about age seven the child emerges from his subjectivity sufficiently to envisage systems of reference that are outside of himself.

Gesell, who has made an extended study of the psychic development of a child's early years, insists on the importance of the seventh year with respect to lying. He remarks that it constitutes a general period of transition when lying is rarer than either before or after this age. Before the age of seven the desire to please and be well considered by his parents dominates a child's sense of the truth. Later lying becomes a function of the increasing autonomy of the self. Before the age of seven, the child lies in order not to lose the love of others and avoid punishment; after the age of seven, he lies for the same reasons but increasingly to augment his power of being, his autonomy, and his freedom.

What follows is Gesell's account of the phases by which a child accedes to a sense of the truth and, consequently, his responsibility toward it. He believes that the child has no conception of the truth before age four.

Age Four:
  • The child tells improbable stories that are often based on reality.
  • The height of imaginative verbalization.
  • Little distinction is made between fiction and fact.
Age Five:
  • Fantastic stories and exaggerations continue, but the child begins to distinguish the true from the

imaginary. He is sometimes aware that he is telling "fibs."

Age Five and One Half:

- Fewer exaggerations and lies. The child sometimes tells improbable stories but usually distinguishes between the real and the imaginary.

Age Six:

- The child denies a fault if he is directly quesioned. Lies are frequently told to avoid censure. Some children are very "honest" in speech but sometimes cheat in other ways.

Age Seven:

- Less lying than at age six.
- Great concern with the evil of lying and cheating, especially when done by the child's friends.
- Quick to report any distortion of the moral code by others.

Age Eight:

- The development of personality goes hand in hand with a tendency to tell lies and boast. But the child distinguishes the real from the imaginary; he may experiment with adults to see whether or not they believe him.

This scheme sets in relief the crucial age of seven when the child becomes "concerned with the evil of lying."

Is this to say that there was no reaction to lying in the preceding stages? No, but the sense of wrong-doing was quite different. It is what Pichon calls "the age of shame."

What is the age of shame? The stage of true guilt is preceded by a stage in which the shame of being discovered predominates. It is not the fact of having lied that justifies remorse; but rather the fact of having been surprised in a flagrant act of lying.

There is no question yet of any reference to absolute truth (and consequently of any absolute understanding of good and evil), but there is reference to the fact of shame in not being able to impose one's truth on others and being found out. Rousseau has pointed out that children are "convinced that they are doing good if we ignore their disobedience."

This is frequently found in primitive mentalities where something is considered a fault only after it is discovered. An undiscovered fault is profitable and is more to be praised than blamed.

Many authorities on primitive peoples have noted that their notion of the true and the false is equivalent to that of success or failure. The liar is one who did not succeed. This is extremely important for an understanding of the archaic sense of truth. It is not the adequation of the mind to the thing; it is rather the adequation of desire to the effect obtained. The primitive sense of truth is reduced to the pleasure principle and the libido. The reality principle, which transcends truth, will only later modify this conception. The classic formula "He takes his desires for realities" reminds us of this way of viewing the truth.

We find an example of this primitive mentality in Jacob's deception of Esau as recounted in Genesis. St. Augustine's celebrated commentary *"non est mendacium sed mysterium"* is scarcely enlightening. Another example is the medieval custom of determining God's judgment by a contest. Success determines the truth: Victory was a sign of God's truth. In this perspective we might say that the true was the strongest truth.

We can easily recognize here the possible genesis of false moral behavior. A successful lie does not imply guilt but a feeling of superiority. A lie that is discovered, on the other hand, engenders a feeling of guilt, failure, shame, and inferiority. A superiority complex or an inferiority complex can quickly result from a fortunate or unfortunate exploitation of a lie. It is evident that a certain worldliness apparently approves of this pseudo-morality that derives from a sense of shame.

At this point we leave the world of childhood. No one would feel guilty if for some good reason he said he was not going to be home at a certain time. But he would be ashamed if, "like a chicken that outwits a fox," he were actually found to be at home.

We touch here on the problem of the quasi-necessity of the social lie and the child, who readily admits the imaginary lie (since the true and the imaginary are fused in a global whole that cannot be reduced to its parts), understands much less evident alterations of the truth, as we shall see in the following pages.

We must now make mention of two essential elements in the discovery of truth: the *intuition of truth* and the *evidence for truth*. Although overwhelmed by his imagination and fantasies, the child nonetheless has an instinct for the truth. Let us recall Bergson's definition of intuition: "By intuition is meant the kind of intellectual sympathy by which one places oneself within an object in order to coincide with what is unique in it and consequently inexpressible." When this intuition of truth bears on judgments as well as things it becomes one with common sense. Common sense is the intuitive divination of the truth.

It is traditional to cite evidence as one of the criteria of truth. How does the child see evidence as the foundation of truth? Is evidence a means for him to discover the truth?

However curious the child may be, he does not question what appears evident to him. Only at a more advanced stage will he begin to doubt, in some cases, the evidence of appearances.

In the beginning his sense of truth does not go beyond perception. That a river, a cloud, steam from a cooking pot, and a snowball are all different states of water is something he will learn later as a result of education. Evidence for a child is what he sees, what he hears and touches as well as what he thinks, feels, and imagines. We might be surprised that he is not troubled by certain phenomena. Suppose that he hears a voice coming from the television set and sees the images on the screen. What does this represent for the child? We are surprised that he finds nothing surprising in this. If he is told that men are speaking "elsewhere" he readily corrects his original impression. Because of a child's capacity not to be surprised he can be easily deceived. All in all, a young child finds the voices emanating from a radio no more or no less mysterious than the gifts he finds under the tree at Christmastime.

A child's sense of evidence is confused with the moral conditions of the superego we have discussed above. "It is evident that such and such is false because I was scolded" and inversely "It is evident that such and such is true because I was rewarded." We find here confirmation of the educative value of sanctions in the discovery of truth.

Conclusion

The discovery of the external world, the confusion of the true and the imaginary, the shame that is experienced when the prohibitions of the superego are transgressed are so many steps toward lying in the full sense of the word. We have seen that intelligence is a condition of lying. But lying in the fullest sense of the word requires that one recognizes the possibility of voluntary negation for a specific end. Thus is structured step by step an adult lie—if we may use that expression—which may be defined as the possibility of denying the truth (by word or some equivalent such as writing or gesturing) with the intention of inducing another into error.

LYING AND NEGATION

Lying is negation and cannot exist independently of negation. To lie is to deny what is, and deny it intentionally. That is to say, with the desire to deceive. We cannot speak of lying without confronting the problem of the origin of negation. We should now like to discuss this problem insofar as it sheds light on the question of lying.

We can study negation from different points of view. We shall be concerned with two approaches here: an existential conception of negation such as that described by Sartre in *Being and Nothingness* and a psychoanalytic conception, particularly the defense mechanisms of the self as described in Anna Freud's works on infantile psychology, which are an extension of her father's thought. Psychoanalytic conceptions are perhaps closer to practical reality. But they do not explain, or only very incompletely, the idea of negation—which is to say the basis and very reality of lying.

All conscious lying supposes an interrogation, a process of reasoning. Even when the lie is spontaneous and intuitive it supposes the subconscious existence of such an interrogation. To lie is first of all to interrogate oneself on the opportuneness of affirming or denying what is. It is at the same time to affirm oneself as the

mediator between the truth and the other, to assume
the liberty of annihilating or deforming that truth.
Lying is the possibility of subjectivizing the truth with
respect to the other by denying his transcendence without being personally deceived. The interrogation that
the possibility of lying supposes is not exactly like
other interrogations. All forms of interrogation suppose the possibility of a negation, but in the case of
lying the interrogation anticipates a negative response.
The interrogation that leads to lying is already marked
by the intentionality of negation. It is no longer an
open interrogation; rather it is an interrogation already
oriented by the liberty of wanting to deny, whether it
be conscious as in the case of habitual lying or more or
less unconscious as in those cases where there is only
partial bad faith. For the sake of convenience we shall
deal with the question of bad faith in a separate chapter, although it is with good reason that Sartre treats
the problem of lying and bad faith immediately after
his chapter on negation and nothingness. Whether it is
a question of lying or of bad faith, there is always
negation. But as Sartre points out: "The lie is a behavior of transcendence." It concerns negation with respect to the other. Bad faith, on the other hand, is a
negation with respect to oneself. It is an attitude of
interiority. It is in some sense the negation introduced
into the very heart of being.

The negation that lying implies is not universal negation. There is a negation for the other but not for
oneself. This is the principal characteristic of lying for
it is a lucid negation. The negation of lying "does not
bear on consciousness itself; it denies only the transcendent." And Sartre adds: "The ideal description of
the liar would be a cynical consciousness, affirming
truth within himself, denying it in his words, and denying that negation as such." Negation for the other but

negation of the negation for oneself. What is extremely important from the ontological point of view is the fact that lying poses the problem of the "for oneself" and the "for the other." Lying supposes the existence of the other: my existence for the other is the existence of the other for me. Sartre adds: "By the lie consciousness affirms that it exists by nature as hidden from the other; it utilizes for its own profit the ontological duality of myself and myself in the eyes of the other."

We have already seen that the discovery of truth necessitated the discovery of one's individuality in a recognized external world. The discovery of negation affirms even more strongly the necessity of the other and our liberty with respect to the other.

The psychoanalytic point of view on negation is not limited to its ontological dimension or, more exactly, falls short of it. We have seen that the notion of truth is marked by the superego and that the child measures his truth against that of his elders either in confrontation or in submission. To please and avoid punishment became two criteria of the true. The psychoanalytic theory of negation is summarized by Anna Freud in the second part of her book where she deals with the defense mechanisms of the self. Negation can be effected by three mechanisms: acts and words, withdrawal into the self, and fantasies. The order we shall adopt differs little from that of Anna Freud because acts and words represent the most normal (or shall we say the least abnormal) processes of negation by lying. The other two are more preneurotic or openly neurotic forms.

Negation by acts and words takes place at several levels, but they all represent the possibility "of retaining the privilege of denying everything that is unpleasant in reality while conserving an exact sense of that reality." This possibility of denying what is unpleasant

becomes confused with the possibility of agreeing with
what is pleasant in fiction. Here we see a difference
between an existential and psychoanalytic conception
of negation. The existential conception is a freedom of
saying yes or no; the Freudian conception is characterized by a rigidity that derives from the determinism of
the libido. Negation by acts and words can take place
in play as well as in the relationships of daily life. In
play, which cannot be equated with lying but which is
nonetheless fiction and unreality, the child acquires
what he does not have but desires; he becomes what he
wants to be but is not. He does not lie, nor does he lie
to himself, even though he is taken in by his game. Let
us recall here what we have said about the contribution
of the imagination to a sense of reality and to the
development of the intelligence. Some of the essential
tenets of the psychoanalytic doctrine are evident in this
phantasmagoria of play in which the child seeks to
become other than what he is, although we must be
careful to avoid hasty or abusive generalizations. The
phenomena of identification with the father, Oedipal
conflicts, and the castration complex are present in
many cases, but they do not explain everything. There
is a form of negation that is based solely on the desire
to avoid immediate unpleasantness. When a mother
asks a child to make his bed or tidy up his room and he
answers that he has already done it (even though he
hasn't), he is motivated by nothing other than the desire to avoid a tedious chore. Whether in play or in the
contacts of daily life, negation of reality by words and
acts represents behavioral patterns that can be judged
normal. But there are other forms of denial that may
seem to differ from the concept of lying although they
are equally a distortion of reality and a flight from the
true. In what Anna Freud calls the withdrawal into the
self, there is a way of denying the truth by refusing to

confront it or by depriving oneself voluntarily or unconsciously of the possibilities of such a confrontation. One does not lie openly but puts oneself in a situation that leads to a distortion of the true and especially to the negation of the possibilities of the true. We find parallel mechanisms with respect to bad faith and would have no difficulty finding others in what is called the hysteria of conversion. Some people afflicted with hysterical paralysis of their limbs are unconsciously trying to avoid an obligation. One of my patients, the sole support of his aged mother, developed paraplegia and could not work. He could not deny his responsibilities toward his mother; but he denied in all good faith the possibility of carrying them out. A child who feels handicapped in some test of strength often consciously (and sometimes unconsciously) takes refuge in lying and thus brings about a temporary inability that enables him to avoid competing with his peers.

There is much evidence to show that withdrawal into self becomes a form of negation that enables one to avoid confrontation with the truth—all the way from the least morbid and most conscious forms to those that are most unconscious and neurotic.[8]

Finally, and still from the psychoanalytic point of view, the last and most neurotic means of negating reality is escape into fantasy, that is to say a more or less radical separation from reality in favor of an imaginary world that frankly bespeaks a neurosis. It may be objected that in some of the examples of withdrawal we have cited, such as hysterical paraplegia, there is an unconscious negation of a personal possibility but no negation of a reality external to the self.

In extreme forms of negation by fantasy there is a radical substitution of the imaginary for the real. This

[8] We shall develop this at length in discussing hysterical lying and simulation.

is not the place to expound a theory of neurosis. Let us merely recall that from a psychoanalytic point of view, all neurosis is a more or less fantastical defense mechanism based upon the refusal (usually unconscious) to face reality. Here again, there are many possible degrees. We shall see the most obvious manifestations when we study reverie, which is a minimal form of self-deception. We shall naturally exclude from our study the most pathological forms that bring about such radical transformation in the person that we can no longer speak of lying.

Psychoanalytic theories are more helpful than others in helping us understand and treat pathological cases. We shall see that they are especially helpful in studying mythomania and neurotic lying, although it seems to us that it would be excessive to apply them to all cases of lying.

2

Lying and Loyalty

WHAT DOES *lying* mean?
 We are not interested in discussing the subject from a moral point of view but rather in sketching a psychological approach to the fact of lying.[1]

[1] The moralists have always been hesitant to formulate a definition of lying because, first of all, a very ancient tradition considered lying "intrinsically evil" and therefore inadmissible, whatever the motives invoked. Secondly, it is commonly admitted that recourse to lying is permissible and even necessary in some cases.

We find a trace of this hesitancy in St. Augustine's comment upon Jacob's lie. He was reluctant to admit that it was a permissible lie and therefore denied that it was a lie at all. *Non est mendacium sed mysterium.*

In this book, with the exception of the reservations noted in this chapter, we shall retain the classic definition. Nonetheless the moralists, out of respect for linguistic clarity and the desire to safeguard the "intrinsically evil" character of lying, sometimes strive in a somewhat acrobatic fashion to say "This is not a lie" in cases where there are good reasons not to speak the truth. In this way they can avoid admitting the possibility of a permissible lie. But this is perhaps a matter of semantics.

But how, then, are we to define a "real lie"? We hold that it is an attack upon loyalty. This position will enable us to offer a more concrete and more precise presentation. That is why the present chapter is entitled "Lying and Loyalty."

To lie is to entertain an untruthful proposition (or the equivalent of a proposition, e.g., writing or a gesture) with the intention of inducing another into error.

Thus there can be no lie without truth and the ability to deny it. That is why in the preceding pages we studied the discovery of truth and negation (which is to say, the power of denying the truth).

But we have also seen that lying supposes an interlocutor, someone who is deceived. Lying is a social and relational act with an external reference.

Moreover, lying has an objective; all normal forms of lying imply intentionality. Lying without a precise intention is almost always pathological, a sickness. This intentionality must be conscious, because if it can be discovered only through psychoanalysis it is pathological lying. Nonpathological lying is a conscious, intentional, and external fact implying a relationship with another. There is no lie that is not a fact of consciousness. "The possibility of lying is given with consciousness itself; it is the measure of the talker's greatness or baseness."[2]

There is no lie if the deception is unconscious. A lie must be distinguished from error. To affirm a falsehood, when we are unaware that it is false, is not a lie. For a long time the child will confuse lying with error because his universe is based on moral pseudoresponsibility. His sense of frankness and loyalty will only gradually become distinguished from other obligations and the world of prohibitions. Lying and falsehood will not in the beginning be very different from one another. Lying requires a certain lucidity, for we can falsify the truth only when we have some understanding of authenticity, of the truth. That is why, as we have said, the age of reason is necessary before we can

[2] Jankelevitch, *Traité des vertus*, p. 236, Bordas, Paris, 1949.

talk of responsible lying. But lucidity of consciousness is not merely a matter of reason; it can be obscured in many ways. We shall see that this clouding of consciousness is one of the essential elements of bad faith as well as lying. Sickness, passion, and fanaticism can annihilate the lucidity that is an indispensable condition of lying. But it is above all the reduction of liberty that is at issue. We cannot lie unless we are free. Here again we must not be misunderstood. What is the minimum of liberty necessary in order for there to be a lie? What is the value (or lack of value) of a lie made by someone who does not have absolute liberty or at least sufficient liberty?

We need not insist on the reality of lying among prisoners, the alienated, and those under torture. But we must realize that lying in its absolute sense is a limited expression of liberty. It represents a superior possibility of the free being to deny what is. "Freedom is free only because it can choose either good or evil; thus the dialectic of lying derives entirely from the abuse of a power that is proper to an adult consciousness."[3]

The possibility of being able to transform the transcendence of what is external to the self as one pleases is perhaps the expression of a deviate freedom, but it is nonetheless an expression that is no longer limited by this transcendence. The freedom of the liar does not make the truth immanent by subjectivizing it, since the liar himself retains a sense of the truth. He cannot even lie freely unless he retains a sense of transcendent truth. The formula of the immanentization of the truth is more applicable to confirmed bad faith.

Lying is the expression of one person's liberty to warp communication between two people. We must consider not only the liar but likewise the one who is

[3] *Ibid.*

deceived, the one who is lied to. Lying cannot be judged outside of the quality of the relationship between the deceiver and the deceived.

An analysis of the fact of lying reveals a person who denatures his own truth in order to transmit it thus falsified to another person who has his own conception of truth. We lie only insofar as we transmit something that is in disagreement with our personal conception of the truth. And we consider ourselves deceived only insofar as we recognize that what we have been told is in disagreement with our personal conception of truth. But lying exists even though the person lied to is not conscious of having been deceived because what he has been told is in general agreement with his personal conception of the truth. We do not have to accept a Pirandello-like universe in which "everyone has his own truth" to realize that the same thing is not seen by everyone at the same time, under the same angle, or with the same eyes.

Our approach to the truth is not the same at all times of our lives or in all situations. But the essential criterion of lying remains the same in all cases: namely, the *intention* that motivates it.[4] The truth of lying, if we may so speak, is the intention to transmit a countertruth, although not an absolute countertruth. Even though the basis of lying resides in its intentionality, its gravity will vary according to the person lied to and the subject lied about. Not eveyone has the same right to the truth and the various forms of lying are not of equal gravity. Frequently a lie is justified for social reasons and no one is deceived. We may be sure that it is not good to tell the whole truth to everyone at all times. The adult understands this very well and does

[4] We cannot disassociate the description of lying from its intention—without which it would not exist—but we shall deal with this point in a special chapter [Chap. 4].

not consider certain deformations or negations of the truth as lying. The child understands this to a far lesser extent; only later will he acquire the critical ability that will enable him to accept certain lies as sociologically necessary without being fooled by them. When, for example, a child calls its mother's attention to a fat lady seated beside them on a bus and says "Look how fat that lady is," he does not understand immediately why this evident truth merits a reprimand. Social life implies the necessity of a certain number of alterations or dissimulations of the truth that have no other purpose than to respect convention. As Goethe said: "In German lying is a form of politeness." The adult's sophistication in this respect frequently disturbs the child who is not attuned to subtleties. I remember the disapproving look of one of my own children when I told him to tell the party on the telephone that I was not in and to call back in an hour. The conventional lie, which is especially inevitable in some professions, sometimes brings about some rather odd consequences. Let me recall here a personal story. For reasons of discretion, my wife has developed the habit of answering the telephone with the words: "This is the secretary." One night at a late hour the phone rang and my wife answered it. The voice on the line said: "Is this Mrs. Eck?" "No," she said in her semiawakened state, "this is Dr. Eck's secretary." The reader can imagine the effect this had!

Sometimes, a lie is simply a way of being charitable. To tell the truth too completely and too brutally for reasons of total frankness could in reality be aggressive and sadistic on the part of someone who uses a concern for the truth as a pretext to express his antisocial attitudes with a good conscience. As Jankelevitch writes: "There is a way of being right that is worse than imposture and calumny. For example, when we deliberately tell a truth that results in someone's death." Some cases raise delicate problems of conscience. Should one tell the truth to those who are mortally ill or should it be kept from them at the price of a charitable lie? This question is so important that we shall devote a special chapter to it [Chap. 9]. Everything depends on what kind of lie it is. The character of the speaker and that of the person spoken to must be taken into consideration as well as the particular circumstances that bear on the right to hear the truth and the eventual right to dissimulate it. The charitable motivation of a lie does not in all cases justify it, because the liar, even though he is well intentioned, always risks falsifying the truth from his own point of view rather than the point of view of the person lied to or in terms of the special circumstances.

One might object that in many cases one is under no obligation to speak and, rather than lying, can always remain silent. This appears an easy way of avoiding responsibility but in fact resolves nothing. Some forms of silence are much more deceptive than a lie. Many think there can be no lie unless it is given verbal or oral expression. This is a normal attitude among children who think that a lie must be formulated; it is also found among adults whose sense of guilt is not aroused unless the lie is expressly formulated. Whatever is not literally expressed does not engage their sense of responsibility, and they are quite unscrupulous with respect to deceitful attitudes, dissimulations, and misleading forms of silence.

LYING AND CHARACTER

Men are not equal in the matter of lying. Not everyone lies with the same facility or the same ability.

Some can lie and convince others that what they are saying is true. But some affirmations betray the lie they are intending to conceal. As Nietzsche pointed out, our words may be deceitful but because of the way we say them we tell the truth anyway. The skilled liar is one capable of lying not only with words but also with his whole being. We cannot smuggle anything by a customs officer who knows we are doing it.

In *The Error of Narcissism* Louis Lavelle insisted on the difficulty many have in lying effectively. "Lying is more difficult than generally thought. The body, voice, eyes, and face are not merely witnesses to but the very essence of lying, and for a keen observer they translate the most secret intentions, even the intention of giving nothing away. . . ."

I myself am evidently not a very good liar. Every time I try to tell some imaginary story at our family table someone always tells me: "You're fibbing." One's eyes especially, and often an imperceptible change in the voice, indicate that we are not being ourselves. We lie more or less skillfully according to our character and ability.

René Le Senne wrote a book about lying and character.[5] In it he endeavored to establish the characterological criteria that motivate one to lie. He considers the essence of lying to be "an imbalance of consciousness that imposes one direction on action while temporarily repressing all others." This means that in some cases, under the influence of an intense drive, the truth can no longer be expressed and it becomes necessary to misrepresent it. Le Senne lists four conditions that favor lying: (1) the narrowing of the field of consciousness, which becomes polarized on a certain point of a situation rather than on the situation as a whole;

[5] René Le Senne, *Le Mensonge et le caractère,* Alcan, 1930.

(2) the intensity of a drive that is awakened by perception and represses other drives even at the price of a countertruth; (3) the general emotional state, which falsifies judgment; and (4) the primacy of immediate impulses, which suppress the rational experience of reflection.

Le Senne is talking here primarily about improvised lies that spring forth spontaneously and suddenly in a given circumstance. A reasoned lie, which is more interesting from a moral point of view, is not included in Le Senne's hypothesis.

It can be readily agreed that a lie spoken spontaneously by someone in a specific situation and under the tension of an oriented consciousness is more the result of emotional impulses than reason. That is why we are rather reluctant to accept a theory of lying based on deterministic characterology that risks limiting or excluding the moral consciousness. The latter cannot be neglected even should we wish to study the phenomenology of lying outside a strictly moral perspective. We have already seen that lying is the expression of a freedom. To try to study it from the point of view of a deterministic characterology would be to overlook this fact.

There is no doubt that some persons have a greater constitutional facility for lying. We can try to understand the liar better in order to grasp more clearly why he lies without excusing or encouraging the act of lying. In his treatise on character Emanuel Mounier is in many respects indebted to Le Senne. He writes: "The emotional type is more disposed than others to lie, but he lies badly. The emotional type is especially exposed by lying, or at least his lie is more apparent because it is improvised and unorganized. Thus he is seen by others in all of his absurdity." The emotional type has difficulty deceiving others, but he deceives himself easily by taking refuge in fictions that charm, nourish, and reassure his emotionality.

The phlegmatic type is not moved by the truth, and he is rarely taken in by the lies of others. He is strong enough to confront the truth directly, rarely lies, and is often capable of being cynical in his use of the truth.

On the other hand, nervous types are naturally inclined to lying. They have an impulsive need to dramatize; but one cannot dramatize without betraying the truth to some extent. If they are gifted with literary or artistic genius, the transposition of their tendency to deform by exaggeration to their works can produce masterpieces. Deprived of genius, their attraction for lying will likely lead them into disastrous situations.

Choleric temperaments do not like to be lied to but are inclined to lie themselves, although explosively and awkwardly, and they are inclined to retract rather quickly.

Active types will lie to the extent that their very activity induces them to do so, while the inactive will not hesitate to have recourse to lying if they think this will lead to peace or enable them to avoid taking initiatives. "The lie that prevents action is one of the constant weapons of the inactive." (E. Mounier)

These types do not exhaust the inventory of character types. But they suffice to show that we are all very different when it comes to lying; we all have different abilities and differ equally in our aptitude for being deceived. The same variations are true with respect to fidelity.

Besides the temperament that predisposes us to lying, are there not personal and constitutional factors that intervene?

It is certain that some children have a greater natural propensity than others to lie or be honest.

Children who are raised in identical conditions can

be extremely different in this respect. It might be objected that even two children of the same family can be in very different situations; one might be more successful than the other; the younger may be jealous of the older, and so forth. One can always find some explanation, but it is certain that there are constitutional factors that predispose one to lying. Hereditary factors are indisputably operative; there are families in which habitual liars have existed for generations. This is true for other defects as well. How often have I heard parents say of their children; "When I was his age I was just like him." We have here the mystery of the undeniable reality of heredity. There are many apparently inexplicable facts. For example, children (as well as adults) who lie only at certain times. At the moment I am treating a child who goes through a crisis of lying every year, usually around Easter time, that is as inexplicable as it is absurd. The crisis usually lasts two months, and the child is exceptionally frank and docile for the rest of the year. I also see adults who periodically fall into a frenzy of dissimulation that is often accompanied by indiscretions in their professional and social life and conjugal infidelity. Here, too, the brutal eruption and passing character of the crisis raises a problem. We cannot speak of an explosion of repressed instincts in a hypermoral temperament. Those afflicted recognize afterward that "they don't know what happened to them." One day there is a sudden awakening with sometimes regrettable consequences. Such episodes must be classified under the category of pathological lies, for it seems clear that they are in fact symptomatic of a periodic psychosis.

Another personal factor that intervenes in the genesis of a lie is that of happiness or unhappiness. We must distinguish two cases. First the child who is unhappy because he is really in circumstances where he cannot be happy. This pertains to the general climate of lying. Secondly, there is the case of the child who feels unhappy although he has no special reason for being so. Often the two factors are closely related, and the inner feeling of unhappiness has a basis in fact but becomes exaggerated, crystallized, and more or less obsessional in the consciousness, feeding more on the imagination than on reality.

We borrow the following two examples from Guy Durandin. Here is the case of a young man who lost his father at the age of twelve. "After my father's violent death we returned to Paris to live with my mother's family. I had lived a very sheltered life, and a stupid teacher gave me a poor welcome when I returned to school. He made fun of me and this disturbed me very much. Although I knew the answer to the question he asked me, I felt nothing but enmity and scoffing indifference for those around me. This happens often. When it came time to return to that class (in which I had the greatest difficulty restraining my tears), knowing the pain I might cause my mother, I postponed telling her about my difficulty and for several days, weeks I believe, I played hooky." The content of this lie is undoubtedly rather banal, but its emotional context is not. We see how this child, who no doubt expected a kind of father substitute in the person of his teacher, was shaken by the latter's mocking attitude to the point where he could not confide in his mother despite his love for her. The lie here does not consist in a real desire to deceive anyone but resulted directly from the feeling of powerlessness the child experienced in being rejected by his teacher.

Here is a case in which loss of affection led the subject to sado-masochistic behavior that took the form of a lie.

A young girl experienced an unhappy love affair.

She was in love with a man who did not tell her he was married and who lied to her about everything. Here is how she described her life after this deception: "At eighteen I told serious lies to two people at once out of weakness. I was unhappy and suffered a great deal. Thus I avenged myself for the deceptions that had been perpetrated on me. I lied to another person I loved very much and manifested great hatred for her."

The girl rightly insisted on the fact that the periods of lying often corresponded to periods of great turmoil in which there was "a loss of emotional security."

However, we must be careful not to reduce lying to a mere consequence of unhappiness.

LOYALTY

We shall see that bad faith is opposed to sincerity while loyalty is opposed to lying. Loyalty and sincerity are neither identical nor contradictory. But they do not correspond exactly to the same criteria.

Sincerity governs my relationship to myself; loyalty governs my relationship to others. Loyalty can appeal to sincerity out of concern for unified moral behavior, but it is above all a virtue that governs social relationships.

Everything that depreciates truth (therefore all lies) is in opposition to the virtue of loyalty. This virtue can be transgressed in many ways depending upon the interlocutor whom the possessor of truth addresses. If I have a negative obligation of "non disloyalty" toward anyone, then the positive obligations implied in my obligation to loyalty can admit of different degrees. It is not my intention here to treat in an exhaustive manner all the moral problems raised by lying, but we cannot deal with the psychological aspects of loyalty without entering into the problems of casuistry that are

raised. Loyalty consists of communicating to an interlocutor that truth to which he has a right. We see here
a new definition of truth that is not based upon the
conformity of language to thought but upon the formula of Grotius:[6] *Negatio veritatis debitae.* To lie is to
refuse to tell the truth to someone who has a right to
hear it. This definition has been generally adopted by
Protestants, except by such rigorists as Kant and
Schopenhauer. There is no need to discuss the moral
aspect of the problem here; rather we are interested in
its psychological aspects. From the psychological point
of view it is clear that Grotius' formula opens the door
to an instinctive tendency to think—if it is opportune
—that the interlocutor does not have a right to the
truth and tempts one to go astray in the underbrush of
mental restrictions. But the moral and social value of
the *veritas debita* cannot be underestimated.

As a professor of ethics has pointed out, we must
distinguish:

Debitum justitiae: we must not refuse to pay our
legitimately incurred debts;

Debitum officii: the truth due to judges or others in
positions of responsibility;

Debitum amicitiae: which consists in not deceiving
those who have placed their trust in us;

Debitum urbanitatis et civilitatis: which requires conformity with customs and social conventions.

This is all rather complicated, but by giving precedence to the notion of the *common good*[7] we may say:

[6] Grotius was a Protestant theologian and jurist. In 1625 he published *De Jure Pacis et Belli.*

[7] The notion of the common good is frequently used today, but it
is not easy to define. Perhaps we can say that the common good represents the totality of the means and conditions that any social group
can and must at any given moment place in the service of all the
members in order that they may attain in a truly human manner the
objective of that group.

Mendacium est falsiloquim communi sensu repro-batum.[8] We are quite aware of the dangers of such a definition. It betrays the kind of thinking, for example, that condemned Galileo. Nonetheless, from a psycho-logical rather than a moral point of view the formula has real value. We must, however, be on our guard against any formula that would cast *a priori* doubt on the veracity of all unusual testimony.

And so we reach a mixed solution, positive rather than negative, to the problem of lying. The solution must reconcile:

the *personal aspect* of loyalty, which is the abso-lute conformity of word or action—or any ex-pression whatsoever—with thought;

the *social aspect*, which relativizes, not the truth which is one, but the communication of the truth in function of a social requirement or general interest.

In practice these two aspects are one, and their agreement forms the very basis of the common good.

I am not obliged to communicate all the truth I possess to another. I would in some cases be disloyal in doing so. It might be a form of indiscretion or, in many cases, a violation of an unconditional obligation to secrecy. To keep the truth for oneself is not to falsify it; it is not to lie. On the contrary, it is in many instances a form of loyalty toward a higher obligation that constrains me to silence.

Loyalty consists in obeying laws among which there is a hierarchy. The law of silence is mandatory far more often than the obligation to reveal the totality of truth.

[8] "Lying is a false manner of speaking that is reproved by the com-mon sense." (Literal translation from St. Augustine: *Contra Menda-cium,* Chap. X.)

All of these problems were dealt with by Jean-Jacques Rousseau in his *Dreamings of a Solitary Walker.* Rousseau was particularly penetrating when he wrote about sincerity. But before discussing this let us pause briefly to consider his general conception of lying.

Rousseau begins his *Dreamings* by recalling how as a child he stole a piece of thread and blamed it on someone else. This insignificant delinquency might be compared to St. Augustine's account of stealing green pears in the *Confessions.* But whereas St. Augustine makes use of an insignificant event to describe the sinner's position before divine transcendence, Rousseau recalls his youthful peccadillo in order to emphasize his arrogant sincerity.

As a result of a basic bad faith that was slowly built up, Rousseau approaches the problems of lying principally from the point of view of the *veritas debita.* But for him *truth that is owed* becomes one with *useful truth,* and he admits that lying about truth that is of no use is permitted: "Truth that is stripped of every possible kind of utility cannot be something owed, and consequently it can be concealed without lying." Further on he attenuates this statement by raising the question: "But are there truths that are so sterile that they are totally useless for everyone?" and he recognizes a transcendence of truth that cannot be violated with impunity even when it seems to have no importance. "Even though I do no harm to my neighbor in deceiving him does it follow that I do not harm myself and is it enough to never be unjust to be always innocent?"

At first sight the moralist may not find anything very significant in Rousseau's meditation on lying. But if viewed in depth we soon see the artificial side of the argument that justifies the arrogant author's narcissistic

and masochistic autoadmiration. It is both a criticism
of lying and an apology for truth woven into the woof
of bad faith.

The dialectic of lying and loyalty is often a sociological problem. All forms of lying are "social." We can lie
or be loyal only with respect to someone or to a situation. There are so many nuances in the transmission of
truth. The euphemism of words, tonality, and gestures
can turn what seems like literal truth into a *de facto*
lie. Inversely, there is a way of telling the truth that in
reality dissimulates it. The dilution of essential truth
amidst a profusion of minor, uninteresting truths is one
such way of lying. This process is common with children who slop an important truth in among a prolixity
of insignificant words in the hopes that it will go unnoticed. Confessors are well aware of the big sin mentioned quickly in a flow of minor accusations. This
process is also exploited in the fine print of insurance
policies and contracts that binds the signatory to
draconian restrictions. The technique is also effectively
employed by advertising companies that give all the
characteristics of a product but put them in such a way
as to leave the potential buyer with a favorable impression. There is also a way of telling the truth that denies
the truth more effectively than if we had lied in the first
place. Sutter gives a good example of this sort of thing.
A diamond dealer was about to leave on a trip to
transact some highly secret business. At the railway
station he meets one of his principal competitors.
"Where are you going?" "To Amsterdam." "Ha! Ha!,"
the other scoffed, "you tell me you are going to Amsterdam so I will think you are going someplace else.
But I know you are going to Amsterdam, so why lie?"

Is it necessary always to tell the truth in order to be
loyal? Isn't there sometimes, apart from the silence that
is more deceptive than speech, the necessity of veiling,

glossing over, adapting, fractionating, and deferring the truth? At bottom what constitutes loyalty is not so much the fact of telling or not telling the truth as the intentions that motivate us. Loyalty is what is due to a given person, at a given time, in a given form, and within given limitations.

But would it not dangerously restrict the concept of lying to reduce it to a mere relationship between the liar and the person lied to? Loyalty is a much broader concept and cannot be disassociated from the common good. Does the fact that X does not transmit the total truth to Y concern only the two protagonists? Won't there often be interferences that make it mandatory to extend loyalty beyond the couple in question? A wife believes out of a sense of loyalty that she must tell her husband that she has been unfaithful to him. But might it not be her duty to remain silent in the greater interest of her family? Indeed might it not be necessary in some circumstances to even deny her suspected transgression in order to avoid dissension that would be a cause of suffering to her husband and children? We shall return to this problem when we talk about lying and fidelity.

Although we do not intend to encroach on the domain of the moralist, it is difficult, with respect to loyalty and lying, to keep from falling into casuistry. This term is often badly understood but means no more than the study of particular cases. And indeed all cases are particular! If casuistry can be abused and lead to regrettable consequences, too strict a coincidence between thinking and speaking likewise leads to impasses. St. Augustine, who was uncompromising on principles, wrote: *Difficillima et latebrosissima quaestio, in qua dissolvenda etiam doctissimi fatigantur.* Without false mental restriction we can say that the virtue of loyalty is not and should not be a static notion, but is rather a dynamic value that cannot be fully realized overnight. It represents a "tension toward" and is intrinsic to all of our efforts to acquire truth. That is why loyalty transcends a one-to-one relationship with another to envisage the *common good*. Our actions and words ought to be part of our pursuit of the common good, which is nothing other than a progressive development of truth. Young people ought to be taught that the problems contingent upon lying and loyalty are not regressively casuistical but are part of the dynamism of expansive charity. The latter can be realized only in sincerity, the *adaequatio mentis secum* that we also find in bad faith: a sincerity whose dynamism is the full realization of oneself. "To become what one is."

These considerations enable us to put two other golden rules of loyalty into perspective: "Say what one thinks" and "Do what one says." These are excellent formulae if they are part of our pursuit for total truth, but they can be dangerous if they serve only to emphasize an isolated truth and soothe our consciences. As Jankelevitch says: "Just because the truth is true one does not necessarily have to say it." And he adds: "Only the *good* is both imperative and normative." The common good is the criterion of loyalty. This notion is more important than the notion of actual truth, and it is only at the point of fulfillment that the good and the true become one. "The veridical man and the juridical man" are not necessarily the same. What confuses the problem is that we too often consider the truth, the true, as that which we think is true without being sure that it is authentically so. Veracity, which is saying what we think is true, must not be confused with truth, which is independent of any idea we may have of it. One duty comes before that of expressing the truth in discourse: the duty of making every effort to make our thinking coincide with the truth. To say what one thinks is a secondary and contingent duty. Our first and essential duty is to make our thinking accord with the truth and an even more fundamental duty is to make ourselves receptive to the truth. But we encounter here the exigencies of sincerity that we shall meet again when we discuss the prophylaxis of lying.

The same problems come up with respect to the formula: "Do what one says" insofar as it is a judicatory element of loyalty. We are now at a third level, that of acting, which comes after thinking and speaking.

We can lie by acting (or not acting) as well as by speaking. This fact highlights the social aspect of lying and loyalty. When we act or refuse to act we more often than not enter into a spiral of irreversible consequences. Our thoughts and words can always be corrected and brought into conformity with truth and loyalty; but to act or refuse to act at the right time in accordance with our thoughts and words tends to be irremediable.

The criterion of truth can be in thought, but it is much more likely to be in facts. Facts have a quality of authenticity that leaves little room for discussion. In saying this, however, we do not mean to deny that speech or even unformulated intentions are without value. To deny the value of *thought* or *speech* would be the negation of a certain interiority; but only when this interiority is confirmed by an external act does it take on its plenitude. Let me refer the reader to a full discussion of this in Hesnard's two books: *L'Univers morbide de la faute* and *Morale sans péché*. These two books demonstrate clearly the extent to which unconscious factors can perturb the notion of responsibility since our conscious motives are not always true. But the danger of Hesnard's theory, from the point of view that interests us here, is his tendency to overestimate action and minimize thought.

Could we conceive of a Gospel that was merely words and not sealed by the Passion and Resurrection? Facts, the created work and the lived, insert truth into time. Words risk becoming mere magic if they are not sooner or later incarnated in action. We lie as much by not acting according to what we think as in acting against what we think. It is better to say "no" and act than to say "yes" and not act. Jankelevitch points out the relevance of the evangelical parable in this respect. "But what think you? A certain man had two sons, and coming to the first, he said: Son, go work today in my vineyard. And he answering, said: I will not. But afterward, being moved with repentance, he went. And coming to the other, he said in like manner. And he answering said: I go, Sir. And he went not. Which of the two did the father's will?" (Matthew 21: 28 ff.) It is better to act according to the truth and the law even though our thoughts and words refuse this truth and law than to boast by our speech or even in our thoughts about the truth and the law and then deny them by our actions.

Is it true, as Jankelevitch points out, that action belies our true intentions? There can be no doubt that it often does, but not always. It is clear that action undertaken according to principles betrays our true interior attitude toward those principles. Action does not lie with respect to principles, but it may lie with respect to our profound conviction about those principles. Does religious practice indicate man's deepest convictions about the Church? I doubt it. The celebrated phrase "I readily believe in the witness of those who die for what they believe" leaves me puzzled. Some no doubt die for their convictions, but I am just as convinced that one can die affirming principles he does not really believe in. We may do this out of pride, but we can also be motivated by fidelity. The true adequation between action and thought is not easily come by, and sometimes action, even the supreme sacrifice, can be in formal contradiction with our deepest feelings. I have known priests who had incontestably lost their faith but who continued in the ministry out of loyalty for those who depended on them. It is possible to sacrifice one's life not out of fidelity to our deepest thoughts but rather out of loyalty for those about us to whom we are united in solidarity. We encounter here that sociological aspect of lying that is the culminating fact. Loyalty toward another, however paradoxical that may be, can sometimes take precedence over what we think is true and even over sincerity toward oneself.

Two examples illustrate the limiting and contradictory forms of this aspect of lying.

The apostate priest, Jury,[9] recounts in his memoires how pride motivated him to continue functioning in the ministry even though he had lost his faith because this provided him with a respectable way of life and in other ways suited his self-interest. The following lines from his journal, written in 1947 when he still kept up the appearances of a believer, are highly revealing. "One is always at war with the Church. And in war one always deceives the enemy and makes every effort to take him by surprise. This is the nature of things. Unfortunately, we must lie; it is absolutely necessary to do so. It would be altogether too cowardly to let victory go to the enemy by default. Let us lie, then, for we will not be more calumniated or dishonored. What shall I lie about? About my true state of mind; this I will reveal in my own good time, when it will be of

---

[9] Paul Jury, *Journal d'un prêtre*, N.R.F., 1956.

maximal advantage for me to do so. Meanwhile, they will believe I am their ally, their servant. Then I will torpedo them." Another priest who confided in me lost his faith a little before the war. But as a prisoner he considered it a duty of loyalty to function as a priest. "The most trying experience of my captivity," he told me, "was the obligation of loyalty that made me do what I didn't believe in because others expected it of me."

These matters will be dealt with in more detail when we discuss sincerity and fidelity.

3

Bad Faith and Sincerity

BAD FAITH

OUR DISCUSSION of truth and negation has shown that lying can exist only in relationship to another.

Lying is an act of exteriority, bearing a necessary relationship to the other. The quality of the other is intrinsic to the very value of lying. Bad faith, on the contrary, is entirely interior; it involves the falsification of the truth, but it is a falsification of one's own truth. Lying is a limited act or a succession of acts and behavior patterns. But bad faith is a state of mind. A lie is something we *do*, but we *are* in bad faith. But before we reach this state there must be, as Sartre points out, "an original intention and project of bad faith."[1] It is important to grasp clearly the different stages of bad faith in order to be able to judge the extent of the responsibility of the person who is in bad faith. In a first movement we project bad faith; in a second

[1] Jean-Paul Sartre, *Being and Nothingness*, trans. Hazel Barnes, p. 49, Philosophical Library, New York, 1956.

movement we are in a state of bad faith. And in a third
movement, it might be said, we use this state to falsify
communication with another. It is important to insist
on the fact that these stages of bad faith can be separated by long intervals. A way of life or a certain kind
of education, for example, might constitute a project of
a state of bad faith that may only much later be externalized. When I say that we "project" bad faith I
should point out that a certain external climate can
contribute to our state of bad faith and consequently
the responsibility for bad faith does not always fall
totally on the subject. To examine the *state* of bad faith
is much more difficult than examining the *fact* of lying.
The moment we knowingly violate our conscience may
be very far removed from the moment when we are
manifestly in a state of bad faith. The genesis and silent
growth of bad faith are often very distinct from its
emergence.

It is in the first stage of the project that bad faith
most resembles lying and then gradually becomes distinct from it. In the beginning "it appears that I must
be in good faith, at least to the extent that I am conscious of my bad faith."[2] Sartre's whole passage on
bad faith would have to be quoted in order to understand his dialectical subtlety. There can be no bad faith
if there is not first of all a cynical attempt to lie to
oneself. Without this first stage of total translucency of
consciousness there would be only error, not bad faith.
If I were ignorant of the reasons behind the Dreyfus
affair I could in good faith be anti-Dreyfus. If I subse-
quently informed myself about the affair yet still
wished to persist in my original attitude, I could remain anti-Dreyfus only in bad faith. When I learn the
truth yet persist in an erroneous state of mind I con-

[2] *Ibid.*

sciously posit a countertruth. The subtleties and ob-
scurities of the mechanisms by which we reach the
state of bad faith raise serious difficulties. Sartre, in his
remarkable analysis, is highly critical of psychoanalytic
theories that attempt to explain bad faith. I myself am
inclined to be less critical of them. There is always an
element of ambiguity in psychoanalysis. Some critics
would say that many psychoanalysts are in a state of
psychoanalytic bad faith, which constantly impels
them to seek justification for their theories. Given the
fact that psychoanalysis makes constant use, and frequently with good reason, of the phenomena of repression, censorship, and the unconscious, some explanation
can always be found for everything. Psychoanalysts
tend to accept whatever conforms to their theories
as evident and beyond question while contrary evidence is written off. The desire to explain everything is
the besetting weakness of psychoanalysis as many practice it.

Bad faith becomes more explicable when a given
subconscious impulse insidiously orients me toward
this or that form of action. If I remain anti-Dreyfus
despite my certainty that Dreyfus is innocent, psychoanalysis will teach me that this attitude of bad faith is
due to the influence of a superego that has been
formed by a patriarchal, reactionary, and anti-Semitic
family from whose influence I cannot free myself. But
psychoanalysis might also make the opposite clear to
me by demonstrating that my anti-Dreyfus attitude of
bad faith is the result of hostility toward a father who
is pro-Semite and anti-nationalist. In this case my hos-
tile attitude toward Dreyfus would be merely a way of
reacting against a castrating father, the result of a deep-
seated Oedipus complex. Of course, the above is a cari-
cature of psychoanalysis. From a psychoanalytic point
of view, when I fall into a state of bad faith it is not

because my ego lied to itself; rather it is because the id (which represents the world of my repressed instincts) deceived my ego.

All of this may seem somewhat beside the point. But it indicates certain practical consequences that are not without importance. While psychoanalysis may be abused and justly criticized for wanting to explain everything, it nonetheless must be credited because of its ability to cure a certain kind of bad faith by making the subject aware of the real motives for his neurotic behavior. Psychoanalysis is of real value in treating some (although not all) forms of pathological bad faith.

On the other hand, I reject the absolutist kind of psychoanalysis that tends to absolve the man in bad faith from responsibility by arguing that he does not lie to himself but rather is lied to. "Thus psychoanalysis substitutes for the notion of bad faith the idea of a lie without a liar; it allows me to understand how it is possible for me to be lied to without lying to myself, since it places me in the same relation to myself that the other is in respect to me; it replaces the duality of the deceiver and the deceived, the essential condition of the lie, by that of the id and the ego."[3] Sartre is rather caustic about psychoanalysis, but he is justified in denouncing a certain verbalism and a certain psychoanalytic mythology that merely displaces the problems without solving them. On the contrary, it makes them esoteric. A certain kind of second-order psychoanalysis refuses to dialogue with those who are not members of the clan. However, I do not accept the following criticism: "Psychoanalysis has not gained anything for us since in order to overcome bad faith, it has established

[3] *Ibid.*, p. 51.

between the unconscious and consciousness an auton-
omous consciousness in bad faith."[4]

It is perfectly true that there can be an unconscious
dynamism that is in bad faith. Freud has given us
ample proofs of this in his discussions of "pleasure
without guilt." Patients often give evidence of the bad
faith of the unconscious. One of my very complicated
and sexually perturbed patients related the following
dream in the course of treatment: He was on a high
mountain road in the company of a number of pretty
girls. At one point the road became so steep that everyone fell to the bottom of the ravine. The rocks and
thorns tore their clothes off, and my naked patient
found himself entangled with his companions, who had
been no less innocently denuded. This recalls the story
of the pastor who always dreamed that a train derail-
ment precipitated the young girl sitting opposite him
into his arms. Obviously the fact that bad faith is
rendered innocent by the unconscious does not explain
it. "How can the repressed drive disguise itself?" Sartre
asks. No psychoanalytic explanation is totally satisfactory. Nonetheless it is a fact.

Here is another example. One of my patients was
treated for an obsessional neurosis that was both scrupulous and sexual in nature. Although she was married
and a mother, she was still a child emotionally. Her
sexual experience was essentially oral, and she found
her greatest pleasure in fellatio. Her guilt over this
nourished her scrupulous neurosis. She often had the
following dream: She died, appeared before the Supreme Judge, and was damned. A devil led her into
hell to suffer the anguish of eternal punishment. She

4 *Ibid.,* p. 53.

was thrown into a pit where she found a multitude of erect, virile objects in which she found her pleasure. She was thus condemned to do what pleased her most for all of eternity. She regularly awakened from this dream covered with perspiration, in a state of acute anxiety combined with erotic pleasure. Her unconscious found a way to enable her to punish herself for what she judged herself guilty of and at the same time satisfy her libido.

I would now like to add a personal dream. Recently I had some difficulty with a person whose friendship I cherish greatly. Some days later I had the following dream: My friend was driving down a steep hill at a high speed. I tried to warn him of the risk he was taking and also tried to stop him. But the car sped onward until it went off the road and crashed. I was in good faith insofar as I did everything possible to prevent the accident. But I also was in subconscious bad faith. This avenged my wounded pride by bringing my friend to his tragic end.

But enough about subconscious bad faith. Let us now discuss bad faith as such.

In his celebrated analysis of the patterns of bad faith Sartre cites the following example:

Take the example of a woman who has consented to go out with a particular man for the first time. She knows very well the intentions that the man who is speaking to her cherishes regarding her. She knows also that it will be necessary sooner or later for her to make a decision. But she does not want to realize the urgency; she concerns herself only with what is respectful and discreet in the attitude of her companion. She does not perceive this conduct as an attempt to achieve what we call "the first approach"; that is, she does not want to see possibilities of temporal development that his conduct presents. She restricts this behavior to what is in the present; she does not wish to read in the phrases that he addresses to her anything other than their explicit meaning. If he says to her "I find you so attractive!" she disarms this phrase of its sexual content; she attaches to the conversation and to the behavior of the speaker the immediate meanings, which she imagines as objective qualities. The man who is speaking to her appears to her sincere and respectful as the table is round or square, as the wall coloring is blue or gray. The qualities thus attached to the person she is listening to are in this way fixed in a permanence like that of things, which is no other than the projection of the strict present of the qualities into the temporal flux. This is because she does not know quite what she wants. She is profoundly aware of the desire that she inspires, but the desire cruel and naked would humiliate and horrify her. Yet she would find no charm in a respect that would be only respect. In order to satisfy her, there must be a feeling that is addressed wholly to her personality—i.e., to her full freedom—and that would be a recognition of her freedom. But at the same time this feeling must be wholly desire; that is, it must address itself to her body as object. This time then she refuses to perceive the desire for what it is; she does not even give it a name; she recognizes it only to the extent that it transcends itself toward admiration, esteem, respect, and that it is wholly absorbed in the more refined forms that it produces, to the extent of no longer figuring anymore as a sort of warmth and density. But then suppose he takes her hand. This act of her companion risks changing the situation by calling for an immediate decision. To leave the hand there is to consent in herself to flirt—to engage herself. To withdraw it is to break the troubled and unstable harmony that gives the hour its charm. The objective is to postpone the moment of decision as long as possible. We know what happens next; the young woman leaves her hand there, but she does not notice that she is leaving it. She does not notice because it happens by chance that she is at this moment all intellect. She draws her companion up to the most lofty regions of sentimental speculation; she speaks of Life, of her life, she shows herself in her essential aspect—a personality, a consciousness. And during this time the divorce of the body from the soul is accomplished; the hand rests inertly between the warm hands of her companion—neither consenting nor resisting—a thing.[5]

Here is another example from my personal files. Mr. X was a good father and husband as well as a convinced Christian. He never thought that he could stray from the straight and narrow and renounce his responsibilities.

One day Mr. X hired a new secretary, twenty years younger than himself and fifteen years younger than his wife. He thought it likely that someone in his office would make advances toward her. But it never crossed his mind that he might be that person. Without becoming immediately aware of what was happening, he began to fall in love with her. He did not recognize, or want to recognize, the changes that were taking place in his attitude. But those around him began to say: "He is not himself." He gradually became aware of what he was doing. But he refused to be totally honest with himself. Another might not hesitate to take the secretary as his mistress and thus more or less deliberately deceive his wife. But to deceive one's wife is to lie and willingly live that lie. Mr. X's conscience would not let him do that. He would not take the secretary as his mistress nor would he deceive his wife. On the other hand, Mr. X began finding fault with his wife, accusing her of a lack of tenderness or of being tender at the wrong time; of not taking care of the children properly (although he had always considered her an excellent mother); of being negligent in her housework, etc. He grew harsh in his speech, which prompted some bitter-sweet remarks on the part of his wife. Mr. X thought: "I must have been terribly blinded by love not to have noticed her faults before." At the same time Mr. X began to criticize his pastor's narrow-mindedness,

[5] *Ibid.*, pp. 55-56.

which he later extended to the Church per se. By degrees he came to think that his personality had been stifled by ignorant parents, an impossible wife, and an outdated religion. No one had ever understood him.

Mr. X had not yet analyzed his intentions toward his secretary in any precise manner. Had he the courage to do so he would have told himself: "Watch out, old boy, you are about to go off the deep end because you want to sleep with your secretary." This would have been sincere, a reflexive insight that would have enabled him to examine his conscience.

Mr. X did not really want to examine his conscience. This would be to admit that he had been lying to himself. He preferred to remain in bad faith and his bad faith gradually convinced him that he was the most unhappy of men, totally misunderstood. He is now convinced that he can fully realize himself only by divorcing his wife and marrying the secretary who understands him. He will do this in all good faith because he has fabricated the justifying arguments.

It is characteristic of bad faith that one lies to oneself so subtly that gradually the lie becomes a new truth. As Sartre points out, bad faith runs the risk of becoming a faith. Bad faith has as an unconscious goal its own end: that is to say, to no longer be a cynical lie to itself. The deceiver, deceiving himself, finally accepts his original bad faith as good faith. This state is not characterized by an essential agreement of his conscience with the truth; rather a good conscience is arrived at by changing the references of truth. Gradually the person in bad faith creates situations in which he can act with the appearances of good faith—so much so that he ends by convincing himself. We could furnish multiple examples of this process. Progressively a situation emerges in which the person who was originally deceived becomes the deceiver. When he encounters those in bad faith, the deceived person can never find a line of resistance to stop his deceiver. He lets himself get caught up in a situation where in the end he appears to be in bad faith because the values of reference have been imperceptibly changed. One has only to recall Sartre's *Dirty Hands*. The character who was sincere in the beginning ended by being suspect.

What is particularly dangerous about the bad faith in which consciousness loses itself in a new faith is that it leads to a loss of a true sense of guilt and often a projection of guilt on the other. We will deal further with this problem in our chapter on witness and confession [Chap. 7].

Does hypocrisy come under the category of bad faith? Yes in one sense and no in another. Hypocrisy is the need to make oneself seem better than one really is; it implies an *a priori* notion of value, which in turn does not imply bad faith even though the latter is not necessarily in contradiction with the notion of value. The hypocrite, we may say, deceives those around him, while the person in bad faith creates a climate in which he deceives himself. Hypocrisy implies an exteriority that does not necessarily imply bad faith. Bad faith can be reinforced by the adjunction of hypocrisy, and hypocrisy can be bad faith. But even so, the two must not be confused. By reason of its exteriority hypocrisy resembles lying much more than bad faith.

SINCERITY

Sincerity, which is the virtue that is opposed to bad faith, is also ambiguous. Sincerity is not truth. In a remarkable analysis J.-M. Le Blond[6] demonstrates

---

[6] J.-M. Le Blond, *Action populaire*, No. 58.

how truth and sincerity can be confused. The truth is external; it is reached by a mental effort. Sincerity can coincide with truth but, as Le Blond points out, it runs the risk of "striking below the belt, appealing more to the emotions that to reason." The orator may be sincere with himself, but "he treats his audience like a flock, more concerned with leading than stimulating thought. Even if he gives his audience the material truth he does not handle it like a truth of reason but like an emotional persuasion in which reason has little part."

Can one always be integrally sincere? Can one sometimes limit sincerity without falling into bad faith? Is it possible to totally avoid bad faith? These questions raise the problem of sincerity, which cannot be separated from bad faith any more than the problem of lying can be separated from loyalty.

There are certain sociological lies that deceive no one; there are also attitudes of nonsincerity that do not deceive and that fall under the category of political or social pseudodemands. We cannot always be exactly what we are and must often adopt the attitude that is expected of us, although this does not make us guilty of bad faith. Sartre gives the example of a café waiter: "Let us consider this waiter in the café. His movement is quick and forward, a little too precise, a little too rapid. He comes toward the patrons with a step and a little too quick. He bends forward a little too eagerly; his voice, his eyes express an interest a little too solicitous for the order of the customer. Finally there he returns, trying to imitate in his walk the inflexible stiffness of some kind of automaton while carrying his tray with the recklessness of a tightrope walker by putting it in a perpetually unstable, perpetually broken equilibrium, which he perpetually reestablishes by a light movement of the arm and hand. All his behavior seems to us a game."[7] If we should meet this same waiter when he is off duty, he would no longer be the same. At home, on holiday, or himself seated in a restaurant the waiter would be a different person.

Can we speak of bad faith with reference to the many roles the same person can play? It is not a question of a lack of sincerity here—simply adaptations of one's behavior to a given situation. In bad faith there is something more: the desire to deceive oneself. I act differently when I receive my patients, drive my car, go on vacation, or paint in my studio. The plurality of roles and activities do not indicate bad faith. I do not deceive myself nor do I try to deceive anyone else. In bad faith, on the other hand, I transform my system of reference in order to deceive myself and thus be able to falsify my judgment about myself and the other's judgment about me.

It is not always the better part of sincerity to remain as one is; it is sometimes opportune to bend to the particular situation. In so doing we need not renounce our personality, dupe ourselves or others.

We also must distinguish two ways of exercising the virtue of sincerity. First of all, sincerity toward oneself (we shall say more on this later); secondly, sincerity toward others.

To transmit the personal message of my sincerity I must always transform it to some appreciable extent in words. All linguistic expression deforms somewhat even as it clarifies. Expressed truth, by the very fact that it is expressed, is necessarily somewhat modified. It is for this reason that artistic expression, symbols, and verbal parables are often more true than the truth that is imprisoned in the carcass of writing.

In a similar fashion sincerity—which is not truth—

---

7 J.-P. Sartre, *op. cit.*, p. 59.

also can be deformed in literary expression. There are few written sincerities that have not been deformed. Sincerity is found much more often in verbal expression, the spontaneity of words, elliptical sentences, and repetitions supported by gestures and facial expressions. People are never exactly what they appear to be in their writings. The latter are never an exact transcript of their sincerity. Consciously or unconsciously something is added to or taken away from it.

There is a certain way of expressing one's sincerity that is only another way of justifying one's own version of the truth rather than seeking the truth itself. True sincerity is "nothing more than consent to the light"[8] —the desire not to be guided solely by one's own light.

There are unfortunately some kinds of "confessions" that are no more than a search for the true in oneself with a corresponding loss of transcendence. This is the error of Narcissus. As Louis Lavelle writes:

"One might say that in contrast to truth, which seeks to conform the act of my consciousness to the spectacle of things, sincerity tries to conform the spectacle that I display to the act of my consciousness. It thus seems that it alone can overcome the duality of subject and object that the philosophers have made the supreme law of all knowledge. Narcissus was damned because he wanted knowledge to be an interior matter. He thought he could see and enjoy himself before acting. He did not have the courage of the incomparable enterprise that precedes being and determines it to a creative unfolding that is symbolized by our interior sincerity."[9]

We cannot be too much on our guard against those "sincere types" who set themselves up as intellectual

[8] Louis Lavelle, *L'Erreur de Narcisse*, Grasset, 1939.
[9] *Ibid.*

masters and lead others along the tortuous paths where they thought they discovered their own sincerity. Gide and Rousseau were such types.

Confessional writings almost necessarily take on a narcissistic quality that stimulates apparent sincerity. The novel becomes for its author a means of being sincere by projecting himself in his hero. Some authors project more than they intend to and are often more sincere by what they unconsciously reveal of themselves than by what they consciously intend.

Too much sincerity with oneself is not always a good thing. Sincerity that is carried to extremes is likely to become an excess of subjectivity.

There is in the excess of sincerity, or at least in what we think is sincerity, an exaltation of the ego that is dangerously close to certain paranoiac attitudes. We cannot denounce too strongly the so-called literature of sincerity, which is no more than an occasion to display what is least good in oneself for reasons of scandal, morbid exhibitionism, or an ambivalent need to simultaneously accuse and absolve oneself because of a kind of sado-masochistic attitude toward society and toward self. For some, moreover, this genre of literature is merely a means of making money and has nothing to do with sincerity. There are Pharisees of vice as there are of virtue. Jean Guitton has written some excellent observations on this theme. "For various reasons we have lost that sense of responsibility borne by one who temporarily possesses a truth that is destined for others. You will say that on the contrary modern man has a keen sense of publicity. Indeed everything has become so public that no one can write a letter or a diary without fearing that it will one day be printed in the newspapers. What modern man has often called *sincerity* is not the effort made to communicate *sincerity* or a truth of which we are the depositary; rather it is the act of unveiling what is mediocre or shameful in our lives, as did Rousseau and Gide, in order to be recognized and to equalize the good and the bad within us. Cynicism replaces hypocrisy for the purpose of putting us at ease in the presence of evil." Such displays of shameless pseudosincerity have an element of proselytism in them and imply the hope of inducing as much as astonishing.

Sincerity may also make us ignore the freedom of the other whom we look upon as a thing rather than a person. We display a domineering ego and refuse to engage in self-criticism, much less accept criticism from others. As Sartre says:

"Thus the essential structure of sincerity does not differ from that of bad faith since the sincere man constitutes himself as what he is in order not to be it. This explains the truth recognized by all that one can fall into bad faith through being sincere. As Valéry pointed out, this is the case with Stendhal. Total, constant sincerity as a constant effort to adhere to oneself is by nature a constant effort to dissociate oneself from oneself. A person frees himself from himself by the very act by which he makes himself an object for himself. To draw up a perpetual inventory of what one is means constantly to redeny oneself and to take refuge in a sphere where one is no longer anything but a pure, free regard."[10] If sincerity is too tainted by subjectivism it leads to paranoid rigidity and a kind of immobilism. The notion of sincerity should not be purely static. It does not mean merely that we should be what we are; it also means that we should become what we are. "Become what you are," said Nietzsche. Sincerity is a series of gains and relapses then new gains. *Itus et reditus,* as Pascal put it.

10 J.-P. Sartre, *op. cit.,* p. 65.

There can be no true sincerity without constant self-criticism, although one should not become immobilized in this perpetual self-interrogation. This would be to replace one abuse with another and substitute for a paranoiac and sadistic consciousness one that is obsessional and masochistic.

So much for philosophical and purely speculative observations. We shall see the educative application of these remarks when we discuss the prophylaxis of lying.

In his *Treatise on the Virtues* Jankelevitch views the problem of sincerity in the perspective of both lying and bad faith. He gives three criteria of sincerity: to say what one thinks, do what one says, and become what one is. The absence of the first two criteria concerns lying more than bad faith. Only the last applies fully to sincerity. Here we must go beyond what we said in our chapter on "Lying and Loyalty." The same problems could have been raised there, but an adequate treatment of sincerity obliges us to transcend the premises we sketched there.

Speech, action, and even repeated lying all take place within a limited time span. Bad faith, on the other hand, is a durable state. What does it mean "to become what one is"? It is to realize little by little one's unity. Perfect sincerity must be in accord with the totality of consciousness. Jankelevitch rightly remarks that sincerity, understood as an adequation of one's intelligence with oneself, would be a simple thing if the self were one. But, he adds: "The self is not an indivisible monad and it is not always in agreement with itself." Would not an immanent sincerity, conceived outside of all relationship with the external world, be a Utopia or a form of alienation? Jacques Rivière[11]

---

[11] Jacques Rivière, *De la sincérité avec soi-même*, Gallimard, 1943.

thinks so and insists on the dynamic rather than the static aspect of sincerity. "Sincerity is a perpetual effort to create one's soul just as it is." He cautions against spontaneity, which is often no more than the froth or moss that floats on the surface and conceals what is in the depths. The bubbles burst and nothing remains of what we thought was our sincerity. Sincerity is ambiguous, as we have already said. We have only to examine it to realize how impossible it is to maintain it. And yet, as Rivière points out, "We do not possess sincerity as something we need only think about once in a while."

Finally, in going beyond spontaneity to the depths of oneself, does not our effort to be sincere expose us to what Rivière calls "the danger of self-integrity"? Who would dare be so perfectly sincere as to reveal the totality of his thoughts? Jacques Rivière to my knowledge was not involved with the psychoanalytic movement, but isn't psychoanalysis precisely this tension toward externalization of everything that is thought? "The soul is full of parodies and demons; it has its monsters and its clowns. Sincerity catches them all in its net along with other prey." Jacques Rivière is in agreement with sound psychoanalytic thinking when he writes that "one should not be honest the way one is blind." I would like to see the whole field of psychoanalysis rethought in terms of Rivière's lucid and unbounded sincerity. "If sincerity confounds our moral precautions," he said, "so much the worse." Sincerity supposes that everything must be recuperated in authenticity, that authenticity that is neither moral conformity nor morbid exhibitionism but a tension toward something. My sincerity is not so much what I am now as a present disponibility toward my future.

Jacques Rivière holds that the essence of sincerity is not only *being* but also *living*. To be sincere is to accept oneself as a living person in a state of perpetual becoming and at the same time to recognize the permanence of the self, which knows how to adapt to events without ever renouncing itself or denying anything. We would have to quote the whole conclusion of Rivière's essay to show how sincerity becomes one with being and life. Then there is no longer any need to speak of sincerity. Sincerity in this respect is like authority. We talk about it only when we do not have it. "I esteem nothing above living and what I want to do primarily is make every effort to live." Dead sincerities sleep on library shelves, shrouded in beautiful phrases and fine bindings. But living sincerity is always on the alert for what can enrich it without ever annihilating it.

The schizophrenic realizes this sincerity with himself because he has cut himself off from external reality. Pushed to the extreme, the dogma of sincerity (considered as the perfect accord of self with self) would be an expression of autism bordering on madness. Sincerity is the accord of the intelligence with everything that constitutes the self, not a self suspended in the void, but one inserted in life and pursuing its fulfillment in unity. This is why bad faith is a state; sincerity, on the other hand, cannot be static without at the same time failing to be sincere. It is dynamic, in movement toward something. Perhaps true sincerity can be found only at the moment of death when all temporal contradictions are effaced and man in completing himself finds his unity.

Sincerity that becomes immobilized in the moment also risks becoming a kind of bad faith: i.e., good faith that is cut off from the past and not projected toward the future.

Bad faith, which according to Jankelevitch is insincerity with oneself, falls between lying and alienation.

But there is a certain sincerity with oneself that is fixed, isolated, abstracted from the real, that becomes, as we have said, a paranoid good faith–bad faith.

Authentic sincerity and good faith mean that we will not admit the possibility of being in bad faith even when we think the contrary.

Bad faith ruins being because it ends by eating away everything. We have said that the first movement of bad faith is a certain consciousness of deceiving oneself. This is less a reflected and voluntary decision than a spontaneous determination of our being. That is why it is easier to be frank than sincere. Frankness involves our will and intelligence; sincerity is a silent disposition of being. "One puts oneself in bad faith as one goes to sleep and one is in bad faith as one dreams. Once this mode of being has been realized, it is difficult to get out of it as to wake oneself up; bad faith is a type of being in the world."[12]

It is a state that conditions us, but it does not involve willing or acting. Authentic sincerity and good faith urge us to admit that our finitude and divided consciousness create a situation in which we can at any moment in all good faith fall into bad faith.

[12] J.-P. Sartre, *op. cit.*, p. 68.

4

The Intentionality
of Lying and Its Climates

THERE CAN BE no lying without the intention to deceive. Prescinding for the moment from the context of moral responsibility, we may say with certainty that the quality of a lie will vary greatly depending on the intention that motivates it and the circumstances attendant upon it.

In this chapter I wish to speak only of normal—that is, nonpathological—lying, which is not subtended by a neurotic state or a collapse of the personality. This does not exclude the possibility that secondary motives, unconsciously close to neurosis, may exercise an influence. Likewise, when we speak of the climate of lying we shall be speaking primarily of ordinary circumstances that affect everyone in every age and only secondarily of exceptional circumstances, although of course we shall not omit mention of the latter completely. In the final section of this chapter we shall discuss the individual and collective character of the fact of deceiving and being deceived.

THE INTENTIONALITY OF LYING

Hell, it is said, is paved with good intentions. Does this popular saying mean that intentions have nothing to do with the gravity of the fault, that only the latter's materiality counts? Certainly not. Lying can be judged only in terms of the intention that motivates it. Nor does this mean that we have only to cover up the deceptive character of good intentions to legitimize them.

We must judge lying in terms of the end consciously pursued by the liar. If we do not bear this in mind we run the risk of being unjust to the pseudoliar.

No countertruth can be good in itself, but the ends pursued in dissimulating and altering the truth can have very different values. The "why" of lying is at least as important if not more important than the "what," "for whom," and "how."

The motives of lying are multiple, and here we shall follow the classification established by the psychologist Guy Durandin.[1] In one way or another the logical lie pursues some end. Only a very feeble-minded liar could be void of all motivation. To say that the lie is utilitarian says nothing about the orientation of its utility. It might be strictly selfish in nature or it may be directed to an end that is not necessarily in the material interest of the liar. Indeed, the lie may be very altruistic.

Let us now consider some examples given by Guy Durandin indicating the different ways in which lying can be motivated.

1. Robert denies that he broke the vase in the living room even though there is no doubt he did. This is the

---

[1] Guy Durandin, *Recherche sur les motifs et les circonstances du mensonge*, Annales médico-psychologiques, 1957.

kind of utilitarian lie intended to avoid punishment. It will be more or less skillful, more or less convincing, more or less tainted with perversity depending on whether or not it seeks to exonerate or to cast suspicion on someone else. Of all lies, the lie to avoid punishment is by far the most common.

2. John knows very well that Robert broke the vase in a fit of anger. Yet he tells his parents that Robert is innocent. This is an altruistic lie, a lie of solidarity. John may later lecture Robert on the importance of telling the truth; but for the moment fraternal solidarity predominates.

3. Christine boasts to her friends of her popularity with boys, a popularity she never enjoyed. She lies, boasts, and bluffs so as not to appear inferior to others. In the beginning this lie may be rather banal, but it indicates a neurosis due to a feeling of frustration, a jealousy of her friends who are more attractive. When does such a lie cease being banal and become clearly pathological?

4. Henry accuses Claude, whom he cannot tolerate, of cheating on his examination. This is false, but he wants to harm someone he regards as an enemy. He is ready to swear that he saw him copying and to furnish proof. This is a lie of calumny intended to harm another. It has many forms of varying degrees of skill and directness. Such a lie would be more serious if, not content to harm directly, it sought in addition to create a climate of discord and suspicion. Adults are more susceptible than children to this kind of lie. An employer who wants to fire one of his foremen will discredit him before his subordinates. He will blame him for all failures and refuse to credit him with any success. He will create a climate of contempt and criticize his foreman's work. The latter, after losing face with his own men, will have no choice but to pack his bags.

He has not been fired; but he has been effectively told to leave voluntarily.

5. Charles is a dedicated member of an athletic team. The latter wins a decisive match on a dubious play. Charles is well aware that the verdict rendered is highly debatable. But he states that everything was normal, that there is no problem. Charles lies to defend the interest of the group to which he belongs, as he would do to defend the interests of his family or his country. He thinks that the general interest is more important than the truth and must be given precedence over it. His lie becomes a matter of passion; it goes beyond particular interest in the name of a falsely conceived general interest accompanied by a bad faith that becomes a pseudo good faith with respect to the general interest. We shall say more about this when we discuss collective lies and attitudes of bad faith.

6. Pierre is timid. To express himself frankly would make him vulnerable. He does not want to appear as he is to his friends. He has neither the conviction of his best intentions nor the courage to admit his weakness, and so he lies to conceal his weakness. He cannot accept himself as others see him not conforming to the group. He boasts of good fortune that he has never had and denies his failings. What is essential for him is to reveal himself to others according to a pre-established plan that will not disturb his relationship with his associates. He is not interested in the truth but rather in a certain utilitarian objective: namely, what he wants others to think of him. On the other hand certain types, dominated by a spirit of independence, will affect an unacceptable image before others. In the one case, personality is dissimulated in order to identify with the group and lose oneself in it; in the other, the purpose is to oppose the group. The essential in both

cases is not to be what the other expects and above all not to be what one is.

This attitude indicates a full-fledged neurotic lie, and we shall say more about it in Chapter 5.

7. Raymond thinks he will never get the money he wants to go to the movies. So he says he needs it to join an organization well regarded by his parents or to subscribe to a magazine he claims is indispensable to his studies. Or he may pretend that he wants to make an offering to the poor. Then, in order to assuage his conscience, he divides the sum in half and at worst can blame himself only for having slightly decreased his contribution to charity.

Raymond lies to obtain what he thought would have been denied him had he spoken the truth.

8. Michael is not fond of Claude. He won't go out of his way to harm him; but neither will he render him the least service. Whenever Claude asks a favor of him he refuses.

9. The same Michael is quizzed by a teacher he fears. He does not know what to answer. The teacher explains and then asks: "Do you understand?" Michael answers in the affirmative even though he has understood nothing. He has lied, theoretically at least. In reality, he dared not contradict someone who intimidated him.

10. Francine loves Gerald. But she fears that her friend Isabel is also in love with him. When talking to Isabel she paints Gerald in a very bad light and says things that are manifestly false. She wants to see how Isabel will react and thus determine whether or not she is a rival. She makes a false allegation in order to get at the truth.

This list of motives is not exhaustive and could be considerably lengthened, particularly with respect to adult lying. Practically speaking, the adult lies for the same reasons the child does. Like children, adults lie to protect and excuse themselves and to harm others; they also lie for reasons of altruism and generosity. Again, like children, adults lie to avoid painful feelings, to hide their inferiorities, to exonerate themselves, to defend their individuality, and to escape from their loneliness.

Sutter[2] insists on a special form of lying among children: the lie that is erected as a barrier against shame. We have seen with E. Pichon[3] that the stage of shame precedes that of culpability, but Sutter rightly shows that the two overlap. We can even say that many adults remain at the stage of shame where the "I haven't seen it, I haven't taken it" mentality dominates their moral lives.

The child lies to escape what is for him a source of shame and primarily to avoid being caught.

As Sutter puts it: "Lying is often a defense against shame. In the stage of shame, vestiges of which remain well beyond the age of seven, evil is any action that is judged reprehensible by adults and a lie can have as its purpose to prevent such a judgment from manifesting itself. The child's elementary ethical sense may also make him experience as shameful everything that makes him different from others—the poverty of his parents, for example, or his lack of knowledge about sexual matters. In such instances the child often tries to give the impression that his family is well off or that he is well informed on the facts of life. Children of an alcoholic parent, a criminal, or an unwed mother, when they are aware of the situation, likewise try, sometimes at the price of the most unlikely lies, to throw others off the scent."

[2] Sutter, *Le Mensonge*, p. 51.
[3] E. Pichon, *Masson édit.*, Paris, 1936.

There is no one motive for lying. A whole complex of motives, including unconscious motives, must be invoked. Some lies are difficult to classify, especially those perpetrated for the purpose of mystification. A special chapter would be called for to deal with farce and irony. Irony even becomes a figure of precious rhetoric both in daily life and in philosophical practice. As Sartre points out, in irony man annihilates in the unity of the same act what he has led others to believe in order not to be believed. He affirms to deny and denies to affirm. Irony excludes bad faith and can even reveal the truth through falsehood. Irony does not imply the intention to deceive and can thus reveal truths that if spoken bluntly would be insulting and unacceptable. Certain forms of irony resemble, although they are not to be identified with, social lies. Irony is as a rule best handled by educated adults, but some behavior patterns in children have a marked ironical dimension to them. There is an amusing case that is a mixture of farce, irony, and mystification as well as utilitarianism.

James is in the seventh grade. He is the only son of very proud parents who themselves are poorly educated. Their son's success in school is their principal concern. Every evening they spend several hours helping him with his lessons. They are amazed at the amount of homework their son brings home every night. Finally discouraged by so much work, James's mother goes to see his teacher and protests. The teacher expresses surprise and soon realizes that James triples the normal assignment. When questioned about this he answered that his parents were so interested in his school work that he increased the amount of homework in order to please them. He even told his mother one day that she would have to buy a rabbit for experimental purposes in preparing his science lessons.

We are expected to know how to kill a rabbit, he explained, and what it looks like inside. His mother followed his instructions. The next day after school his father asked: "How did the lesson on the rabbit go?" James answered: "There was no lesson on the rabbit. I just wanted to know how it was done."

We cannot leave the subject of the intentionality of lying without briefly discussing the problem of how the moral conscience reacts to lying. Attitudes here vary greatly depending on the ages and circumstances of those who exercise "the ability to lie."

A statistical survey indicates in a very interesting fashion how different kinds of lies are judged.

The lie of calumny is the most despised.

The lie to avoid punishment is almost universally forgiven. The more personal interest (which is a measure of primary intentionality) is involved, the more serious the fault is considered. Furthermore, the protective lie to avoid punishment is interpreted in widely diverse ways. We shall have to discuss this at greater length later on because sanction, the corollary of lying, indicates the quality of the person lied to and his capacity for handing out punishment. There is no doubt that lying implies personal guilt. But the full existential nature of lying further supposes the presence of another who has the right to the truth and therefore the right to sanction the liar. It is always difficult to disassociate lying from a master-slave dialectic and look upon it as a problem of conscience vis-à-vis an absolute.

The adult judges the liar severely but is more tolerant of his own lies. He does not like to be caught in the act of lying, and his lie pertains much more to bad faith than to lying as such. He is inclined to forgive lies and deceitful behavior when they help him succeed. He will not admit that he lies but thinks himself rather clever for having said or not said a certain thing. He forgets that there are lies of omission and that loyalty can be transgressed as much by not speaking the truth when the interlocutor has a right to it as by falsifying it. The adult perhaps lies as much as the child, but he is more reluctant to admit it. According to confessors, children accuse themselves of lying much more than do adults.

The child is not so inclined to see justifying and exonerating circumstances as is an adult. His incipient conscience does not make much distinction between the different degrees of lying. He says something that is not true. That is all; he seeks no further explanation. This is due to a certain moral formalism in the child who has not yet been instructed or has been poorly instructed on the notion of responsibility. He has been taught a formal morality that takes into account only the act and not its intention or consequences. But the finer moral sense required here is obviously difficult to acquire.

An important study by G. H. Wallon[4] shows that the notions of wickedness and dishonesty become associated with lying relatively late in a child's development, not to be found before the age of seven. This is not surprising in light of what we have said about the development of the sense of truth before this time. What is more surprising is that very few children before the age of fifteen count lying as a reprehensible act.

The child almost always regards lying as an immoral act but accepts it as a necessary way of life in order to protect himself and live in peace. He sees lying more as a violation of social conventions than as a veritable fault. Sutter says on this subject: "When a child lies in

4 G. H. Wallon, *Les Notions morales chez l'enfant*, P.U.F., 1949.

a concrete situation he regards his act as a form of social behavior since he considers it, and rightly so, as a means of adapting to society. His behavior is at least in part motivated by society. He is no doubt aware that his act is also called a lie, but almost all lies seem to him excusable. He does not identify them absolutely with the lie he has learned to judge reprehensible."

All of this implies educative consequences, the most important of which is the necessity of a positive rather than a negative education. To tell the child he must not lie is less meaningful than to teach him to be loyal and to love the truth. We shall return to this in our discussion on the prevention of lying.

Lying is the most subtle way of entering into a parallel moral life by reason of the fact that it does not initially seem fundamentally serious. The nonpathological lie becomes the means and not the end of moral deviations. It is utilized as a pseudoexcuse for numerous behavioral problems. The pure liar is an exception, the case of mythomania apart. Lying is looked upon as a minor fault, yet it opens the door to more serious deviations later on.

The child can be judged on the frequency, importance, and motives of lying more than on his other faults such as disobedience, anger, and pride. Lying also serves as a basis for judging the educative value of parents and teachers: However, lying is more often than not a servant of other faults, a servant that they cannot dispense with. This is more true for the child than the adult, who has more freedom and therefore less need to dissimulate.

In his study on lying Guy Durandin, after evaluating how the child judges the moral value of lying in light of his intentions, tries to determine how individual lying compares with lying perpetrated by another. Are *lying* and the *person lied to* judged in the same way?

His study shows that in general the subjects consulted were less pessimistic in judging their own tendency to lie than that of others. In other words, we more readily suspect others of being capable of lying than oneself.

What is particularly interesting in Durandin's study is that lying to protect the person is judged in an identical fashion whether it be a question of one's own person or another's.

A lie to protect one's privacy and self-integrity is a very common way of altering the truth. This is a utilitarian lie but a very special one, for it is at once a defensive and aggressive reaction: One lies to protect one's person but one would also lie to penetrate the other's secret. Durandin gives the following example. "A young woman of twenty distinguished different periods of her life. Some of them were characterized by lying, others not. She lied very little until she was around fourteen or fifteen. Then, she said, 'I lied to my parents to hide myself from them. I thought that they did not understand me.' She then described her present situation. 'I do not lie to my friends and very little to those persons I trust, although the latter are rare, perhaps five in all. I lie a good deal to those from whom I want to hide my life or rather those I do not want to be part of my life.' What is important about this young woman's way of lying is that she does not try to obtain this or that result but rather to protect herself in a general and so to speak instinctive way from intrusion by others."

The lie to protect one's person may be related to a very real concern for sincerity. The excessive fear of not being sincere with oneself by letting others invade one's life can tempt one to lie. Durandin rightly insists on the ambivalent, dialectical aspect of this kind of lie. The liar then "manifests a desire, sometimes even a need, to be loved for what he is. If people could be assured of being loved in revealing themselves to others as they are, they would no longer feel obliged to hide their personalities as they do. Thus the fact of hiding our personality indicates both the fear of being known and the desire to be known, but known by someone who approves, loves, and, if possible, helps us. What at first seems contradictory from a strictly logical point of view—the desire to be at once known and not known—is not contradictory when the two attitudes are viewed in context: We want to be known only to the extent that being known signifies being loved, and we refuse to be known insofar as being known would signify being used."

THE SOURCES AND CLIMATE OF LYING

When adults speak of lying they always give the impression that only children are guilty of it but not them. Parents readily agree that the duty to truth is different for adults and children, but they are convinced that in practice only children fail in this duty. Adults pass judgment on the truth that is their due without for a moment thinking that they too lie and, more frequently, create the climate in which it is impossible not to lie.

To lie is to have the intention to deceive. But there are situations in which the intention to deceive becomes an almost compelling obligation. Are we adults, parents, and educators always sure that we speak the truth and make truth possible for those who demand it of us? The obligations of life force us to admit a certain relativity of truth and likewise a relativity in our duty to communicate it. Lying may be excused by social necessity but, as we have seen, in this case no one is deceived. A society in which all truths were bluntly exposed would be more like a hell than a paradise.

Not to speak the truth is sometimes a duty. To want to be perfectly sincere is not always to be loyal and charitable. To take refuge behind the obligation of telling the truth is sometimes to assuage one's conscience for being cruel.

When X, under the pretext that he can no longer hide the truth, tells his wife that twenty years ago he deceived her with another woman, we may be quite sure that his urge to tell the truth was primarily a desire to hurt his wife.

A certain mother who is totally deaf cannot help repeating to her children that they are responsible for her deafness. This is literally true and all ear specialists know of many analogous examples. She tells this to her children with much apparent circumspection but believes that in the name of truth they ought to know they caused her deafness. One of them recently attempted suicide because he could not tolerate the idea of being responsible for his mother's infirmity. What was the duty to truth in the above two cases? Was it conjugal love, maternal love, or the bare truth abstracted from any reference to love? There would have been more real truth in silence than in words.

It is certain from the moral point of view that it is easier to formulate a law of silence than the law of a necessary countertruth. I leave it to the moralists to determine whether or not there are cases that legitimize a certain duty to falsify the truth, a duty that goes beyond that of remaining silent. This is a difficult question and I have no competence to discuss it. What more or less ignored motives can assuage the conscience of one who hides or denatures the truth? Can

we be in good faith when we do it? And to what extent
did we reach this state in denaturing by special artifices
what was in the beginning only bad faith?

If we except the evident cases in which the adult
deliberately lies and deceives in order to benefit by his
disloyalty, then the essence of adult lying would appear
to be bad faith.

There would seem to be a direct parallel between the
lies of youth and the bad faith of adults, the lies of the
child and the bad faith of parents. Children acquire the
need to justify their lies only later on. The adult is
much more frequently concerned with assuaging his
conscience and the road to a good conscience at the
price of lying passes through bad faith.

We come now to the confrontation between the
deceiver and the deceived, to the interpersonal relationship. We do not mean to establish a one-way relationship between the lying child and the deceived parents.
Adult lies to children must not be underestimated. The
parent-child relationship in communicating the truth
must be reciprocal. The adult lie, subtle as it may often
be, leads inevitably to the child's lie. The adult's malice
and cleverness in deception will be so many lessons in
expertise for the child. When parents are caught out in
a lie there is little they can say when their children lie.
"To each the liars he deserves." (Jankelevitch)

It might be objected that the unity and absoluteness
of truth has nothing to do with the moral use that is
made of it. But it is certain that when a father cheats
in his business and boasts openly about it before his
children, he will have great difficulty in getting them to
be perfectly sincere or to feel guilty about their own
disloyalty. Some years ago I treated a seventeen-year-
old boy. He had been referred to me by his parents
because of his constant lying. The boy told me he
worked with his father.

"What does your father do?"

"He sells cars."

"How do you help him?"

"I renovate the cars."

I asked him how he did this. He then told me that he turned back the speedometer, used a special high-powered gas, and the like. Yet his father, who made him do this work, was highly displeased when his son lied to him!

A mother brought her daughter to me for consultation because she lied constantly, inventing highly imaginative stories to explain her tardiness and absences from school. When I talked to her, the girl told me that her mother was deceiving her father and often asked her to fabricate alibis. The girl complained to her mother, but the latter would put her off with the words: "You will see how it is when you are my age and have lived a little."

I recently treated an adopted child. All of his troubles stemmed from a situation that he suspected but that his parents had never talked about. They had told him he was their natural child and did everything to make him believe this. But he doubted this was the case. When I talked to him I had the impression that he knew exactly who he was. I told this to his parents. In my presence they questioned the child, who answered: "I have known for a long time." The angry parents then exclaimed: "What! You little liar! You knew we weren't telling you the truth and didn't tell us!"

Stories about Santa Claus and devils with horns are so many countertruths that falsify the child's mind—not only the substance but also the formal expression of the truth. The many erroneous affirmations and imaginary tales indulged in by parents and grandparents are not apt to give the child a sense of authenticity. Unfortunately, religious imagery is often a part of all this. But let us not be too harsh. We shall see that myth and the imaginary can have positive value.

Whenever truth is not an equal exchange it is a source of lying. The child, understandably enough, cannot grasp how there can be two truths: one obligatory for him and the other, much more relative, for adults. In Kafka's celebrated letter to his father we find an expression of the crushing inequality between child and adult with respect to the truth. If a child lacks the certainty that his obligations refer to the same moral system as those of his parents, if he feels that the latter relativize truth in terms of their interests and do not believe in truth as such, he too will construct a system of references to justify his own interests.

The limit of obligation to the truth is often difficult to specify in parent-children relationships (which are bilateral rather than unilateral). To what extent are both obliged to speak the whole truth? A climate of freedom must be created in which the whole truth can be spoken even though there is no obligation to tell everything.

The obligation to tell the whole truth would soon result in a violation of the child's conscience and lead to that form of lying whose primary intention is to preserve one's person and privacy.

Parents who act like inquisitors would almost necessarily cause their children to dissimulate, for only at this price can they be themselves.

Another attitude encourages children to lie. It consists in systematically suspecting them of lying. "Why should I tell the truth since no matter what I say no one believes me," a sixteen-year-old boy told me recently. His mother always doubted everything he said and cross-examined him even in unimportant things. She treated truth and falsehood in the same way.

In many cases, the parent-child relationship exists solely on the plane of accusation and defense. Such families are like police courts. When the child knows that he will inevitably be accused and condemned, that the confession of his mistakes and peccadilloes will automatically bring about punishment, he will take refuge in lies. Regularly caught out in his attempts to conceal or falsify the truth, he will give cause for new sanctions and so the infernal circle continues.

To what extent should we encourage the child—who knows that he will be punished for any confession of lying—to keep silent about his lies or exaggerate them? There is no court of law in which the judge has the right to demand the defendant to tell the truth or punish him if he refuses to tell it. This is part of the defendant's right. All jurisdictions—even the canonical —recognize this right and the accused never swears to speak the truth. If a child is always presumed guilty, does he not have the right to avail himself of the privilege of defense?

We have insisted on the importance of weighing intentionality in judging lying. It is just as important to weigh the climate in which communication between the liar and the deceived is established. Often enough lying stems directly from the bad quality of this climate. Before accusing our children of being perpetual liars we should examine our consciences and ask ourselves whether or not we have created a climate in which truth is possible. In some climates truth easily takes its course; in others, truth is impossible to the point where it assumes the guise of falsehood.

The climate in which truth takes its course is not always created by families in which total frankness prevails. To tell everything is often a way of telling nothing. There can be an abusive way of telling the truth that amounts to concealing it. Exaggerated stress on details that are in themselves true can be a technique for concealing the essential by drowning it in a torrent of unimportant truths. "Small truths distributed drop by drop also serve as an alibi for big lies." (Jankelevitch)

It is sometimes better to say nothing than to say too much or too little. Adolescents always think they must answer whatever question is put to them. Parents would be well advised not to ask too many questions, especially when they are pointless or will necessarily evince a deliberately false or incomplete answer. The repetition of certain indiscreet questions leads to the repetition of certain false answers.

My father was the best and least inquisitive of fathers. He respected the autonomy of his children and never asked indiscreet questions. But if he heard one of his children coming home late at night he could not help asking: "What time is it?" This question always bothered me, although in reality my father wanted to know how much time he had left to sleep rather than to control the nocturnal activities of his children. Eventually I stopped giving him a precise answer and would say: "It is a quarter to" or "It is half past the hour." My father was reassured by such an answer and went back to sleep. The next day he would be the first to laugh at our little joke.

Many parents are reluctant to grant their children the right not to say everything and do not understand the necessity of respecting their privacy. There is a way of not saying everything that perfectly safeguards the parents' right to the truth. There is a hierarchy in the truths that must be told and those that it is possible not to tell. We should impress upon the child that he is dishonest in concealing some things even though the exigencies of loyalty do not oblige him to tell some others. My children do not show me their school marks every week, but every time one of them has had a bad mark he has told me voluntarily.

When lying threatens to contaminate a relationship, reciprocal trust and recognition of the other's good faith makes it easy to tell the truth.

Good faith supposes that each of the two parties admits the possibility of deception or error from the outset. In these conditions, dialogue is not the demand for or the duty to truth; rather it is a common search for the truth that is a very different matter. Without altering its character, we must conceive of truth dynamically. The search for the truth, the march toward truth, even though it sometimes involves error, is already truth.

The climates of lying and bad faith characterize all forms of human society, beginning with that basic society that is the couple. The climate in which a couple lives completely conditions the possibilities of loyalty, sincerity, and to the extent that this climate borders on lying and bad faith it invites infidelity, deception, and adultery. We shall study in another chapter the relationship between fidelity and lying.

What climates will open the road to lying and infidelity? They are essentially two extreme aspects of the couple's life. On the one hand, a totally independent existence, the juxtaposition of two lives, in which one does not live for the other and reciprocally. In this case the unity of the couple is nothing more than a perpetual duality. Each partner has his life, his personal outlook and obligations. There are moments of intimacy; an effort is made to reach an understanding on certain key issues, although these are usually more negative than positive since the main concern is to avoid interfering with one another's life. When this simple juxtaposition corresponds to what the two protagonists want there is little difficulty and no one suffers. Lying isn't even useful since the other is not considered as one having the right to the truth. When deception occurs no one is, as a rule, deceived; all that is asked is that neither be too unreasonable and that there be no embarrassing social incidents. The situation becomes rapidly explosive and requires lying when only one of the partners desires this way of life. In this case the party desirous of independence must either dissolve the relationship or resort to lying.

In the second instance, the couple wants to share everything and tell everything, leaving no room for independence or liberty. Neither partner can have any privacy, special pursuits or friendships. In the end, everything in the other is rejected that does not come from oneself. Little by little, everything that differentiates the couple is eliminated. Jealousy sets in. It becomes difficult to breathe and when the atmosphere becomes too stifling the only escape is by lying. One must seek fresh air on the outside, but since this must be kept a secret from the other, one invents any lie whatsoever.

In addition to these extreme climates there are relative approximations that gradually constitute an atmosphere that might be described as the antichamber of lying and betrayal. Morbid jealousy especially leads to undesirable consequences. The jealous person is in bad faith vis-à-vis the person he is jealous of and vice versa. One who is wrongly accused by a jealous partner may soon come to think that he or she might as well provide a motive for the accusation.

In other cases a whole chain of annoyances can make life impossible for the husband who returns exhausted from the day's work. If he resorts to the lie of adultery it may be less to deceive his wife than to pass a few moments with someone whose company he enjoys. Women who are domestic tyrants are not the only ones who drive their husbands to bad faith. The wife who feels neglected by her husband, who considers her a mere servant of his needs, will also often be tempted to a similar lie.

THE CLIMATES OF EXTRAFAMILIAL LIES

Business associations may be characterized by frankness or insincerity. In some establishments the employees are happy because a climate of frankness reigns; others are stifling because a climate of bad faith is dominant. The managers are essentially responsible for the climate that prevails in a business operation. If the owner himself is frank, the general atmosphere of his business will be open. If he is devious and in bad faith, this spirit will reverberate at all levels. Often an incompetent owner will resort to lying and bad faith in order to impose an authority he does not have. It is usually those without authority who complain most vociferously about its breakdown. A strong man can afford to be honest. I do not totally share Detoeuf's opinion that he puts in the mouth of Barenton in *Propos d'un confiseur:* "The courage of lying is not given to everyone. It is not only honest folk who always tell the truth. The weak and timid do also." I think that as a rule the weakness and timidity of leaders rather than their strength lead to lying. And when the vanity and pride of mediocrity are added to his incompetence, weakness, fear, and bad faith, then the business leader risks taking measures that will jeopardize his enterprise. It will become almost impossible for him to admit his error. Too cowardly to confront his subordinates, he will try to create an atmosphere that will oblige them to leave of their own initiative.

We cannot in this essay review all the ways in which

lying contaminates the various levels of society. There are passionate collective climates that engender bad faith in whole groups. There is the lie of the politician who disguises the truth in order to confuse the issues or presents the truth in such a way that adherence to it is no longer free. There is a certain way of asking questions that is deceptive. There are also the lies of one nation to another and the bad faith of a group of nations toward another group. There are collective climates of extortion and business dealings that constantly distort the truth and put the appearance of truth in the service of ideologies.

My experience as a psychiatrist, which began more than twenty-five years ago, included the period of the German occupation. During that time children who could not distinguish between legal authority and the truth certainly had their conception of loyalty and their emerging moral sense distorted. What family did not listen to the forbidden English radio! But this could never be admitted. What family could not boast of having obtained foodstuffs without ration coupons? Those who were most scrupulous with respect to money became openly lax when it came to that other money known as ration booklets. Children could not make the distinction between these two currencies. I remember seeing on Christmas eve of 1944 my little girl admiring a beautiful doll in a store window. She caught her mother by the coatsleeves and said: "Go get some money and some coupons." This was a terrible period for the moral formation of the very young.

5

The Pathological Lie
and Its Limits

IT IS TRADITIONAL to oppose a "sick lie" to what might be called a social lie (since it is rather awkward to use the expression "normal lie").

The limits between the different categories of lies are fluid and very artificial. We must also take note of pathological forms of sincerity. Alcestis is not very normal and the sympathetic Cyrano, who always tells the truth, is highly neurotic. As for Jean-Jacques Rousseau, his deliberate sincerity is not always very healthy.

The pathological lie falls into the larger category of troubles of the imagination. Here we shall not be concerned with those troubles of the imagination that correspond to profound alterations in the way one thinks or in one's personality. Imaginary madness is not part of the study of lying since the madman believes in his madness. The delirious megalomania of the paralytic has nothing to do with that of the mythomaniac. We shall also omit consideration of certain oneiric states and certain confusions. On the other hand, we shall study reverie, which in some respects falls outside of lying, bad faith, and truth.

MYTHOMANIA

Mythomania is a large chapter in the book of pathological lying. This does not imply that it is easy to characterize it. There is no well-defined mythomaniacal sickness; it can take very different forms depending on the subject.

The child has a natural inclination to mythomania, although there is no question of pathology in this case. Dupré speaks of the normal mythomania of the child. Mythomania is independent of one's level of intelligence. Those afflicted with it are more or less subtle, more or less intelligent; that is all we can say. They may be perverts, but not necessarily. They can also be altruistic and generous. There are sadistic and destructive mythomaniacs. Hyper-moralism can subtend mythomania as well as cynicism and perversity. Traditionally, girls have been considered more inclined to mythomania than boys, although the opposite is often the case. Incoherence is more damaging to the male sex than the feminine. A female mythomaniac takes more risks and is less abashed before the improbable than the male mythomaniac. Woman is the tightrope-walker of mythomania, while man is the jobbing workman. A sophisticated author of the *Belle Époque* said that women are the aristocrats of lying while men are the commoners. Lucienne will not hesitate to say that her car can go from Paris to Marseilles in only six hours; Raymond will bluff but will instinctively pay more heed to how the car can actually perform. A girl's mythomania will be eloquent and sentimentally persuasive; a boy's will be more modest. One will say:

"Believe me." The other will say: "You may believe me." But there is nothing absolute here and male and female ways of denying, affirming, inventing, and dreaming are often interchangeable. A girl's mythomania more readily tends to the absurdity of the gratuitous statement; a boy will try to make his lie seem logical. A girl unconsciously thinks: "It is important that I draw attention to myself no matter what." A boy will naturally try to make himself appear superior in the eyes of others. A girl will take pleasure in telling stories about how her gracious person was the object of outrages, especially when a brief description of the latter increases the attention paid to her. A boy will be more likely to insist upon the fierce resistance of the pretended victim to his indisputable powers of seduction, which finally triumph. He will never invent a story in which he is constrained to satisfy the white-hot lust of a middle-aged woman. If he thinks of himself as a victim of sexual aggression it will be that of another male, and his struggle will be decorated with the medal of resistance to immoral and unnatural propositions.

If I may judge from my long experience as a child psychiatrist, I would say that mythomania is equally divided between the sexes although it should be borne in mind that I see roughly twice as many boys as girls. If the problem is envisaged from the point of view of a Ulysses-like craftiness, then the palm goes to boys; but the inverse tends to obtain in the case of adults. At this level the feminine sex occupies a privileged place in the world of fabrication.

Dupré gives this definition of mythomania: "A pathological tendency, which is more or less voluntary and conscious, to lying and the creation of imaginary fables." I am in full agreement with this definition, although everything turns on the "more or less." Let us note that there must be "less" rather than "more" if we are to speak of mythomania, because it would not exist if it were perfectly conscious and voluntary.

Dupré observes that the tendency to create imaginary fables is externalized in the form of oral recitation or writings and can be accompanied by considerable bravura. One cannot be a mythomaniac under just any circumstances; a favorable atmosphere is necessary that is characterized by what we have described as the climate of lying. A durable personal inclination is also required. There can be occasional mythomaniacs who construct their fabrications for a limited time, in the context of a given situation or for reasons of a temporary necessity. But they can hardly be called mythomaniacs even though the tangle of events may lead the pseudomythomaniac to continue lying indefinitely.

The true mythomaniac constructs a coherent story (coherent for himself at least) that he tries to make others believe. He ends by believing in his own fabrication, and this in the measure that those around him believe it. He is a gambler who doubles his wager every time he sounds a note of credibility in others. The mythomaniac will not cease lying out of a desire to be truthful. He will cease only when he thinks it no longer has any interest or when he has been found out. He will then construct a new fabrication. The mythomaniac is not necessarily in search of a project. He seeks to satisfy a drive that can be oriented in any direction whatsoever and indeed can work to his disadvantage. The psychoanalyst can find profound reasons for these diverse orientations of mythomania: sadism, masochism, etc. But he is usually motivated by a desire to play a role; there is a kind of theatrical exhibitionism in the mythomaniac. This desire often stems from a comic sense but can end in tragedy. Nothing is more baffling for the observer or therapist than the mythomaniac's behavior. When discovered, he retains his composure. If he is backed to the wall and has nothing more to invent he will dramatize out of the need to play a role. P. F. Girard, in a chapter on mythomania in his book on childhood irregularities,[1] emphasizes this fact: "He [the mythomaniac] plays the role of a penitent, pretending that he will begin afresh; he is at pains to explain why he tells stories. In explaining why he was forced to conceal the truth he begins a new fabrication even more astonishing than the first." In mythomania the desire to attract attention takes precedence over the desire to deceive. Here is an example of mythomaniacal fabrication that seems unlikely, but I can guarantee its authenticity.

A certain Miss X is a professor in a liberal arts college. She has just turned thirty. She is bothered by her celibate condition less for reasons of passion and the need for affection than because two of her younger colleagues recently married. From a natural point of view both of these girls were less pretty, less intelligent, less able to make a man happy. Things shouldn't be like that!

Miss X returned from the Easter holidays radiating joy and disporting an expensive diamond that was bought in Burma. She announced her engagement to a distant cousin who, as though by chance, had the same name as she. The marriage was scheduled to take place over the summer holidays, on the estate of her pseudo-fiancé. When she returned to the college in the fall Miss X's eyes had that special look of a fulfilled bride. Her colleagues extended felicitations. They were anxious to meet her husband and many social invitations were extended. Miss X offered endless explanations to the effect that her hasband—a much-decorated military officer—was engaged in highly classified work and had

[1] P. F. Girard, *L'Enfance irrégulière*, Psychologie clinique, P.U.F., 1946.

to travel a great deal. She received the customary sympathy reserved for young brides who must be separated from their husbands. Visitors to her apartment noticed that a large double bed had replaced the cot of her single days.

But after a while Miss X came to realize that an imaginary husband is a cumbersome commodity, even though she thought she had anticipated every possible difficulty.

One evening the young bride decided to rid herself of her fictitious husband. What would be the best course of action? Divorce? She didn't believe in this and furthermore was afraid of how it would affect her position at the school. Death? Yes, she could make this credible. She let it out that her husband had terminal cancer. Each morning she would come to work with the ravaged face of a wife who has spent the night at the bedside of her dying husband.

Her colleagues showered her with sympathy and each morning inquired solicitously about her husband's health. Everyone followed step by step the long calvary of a young woman about to lose her husband so soon after marriage and without the prospect of motherhood.

Of course, sooner or later death had to terminate this horrible adventure. And at this point Miss X's carefully constructed fable collapsed. In real-life crimes the embarrassing give-away is the cadaver. In this case the absence of a cadaver proved to be Miss X's downfall. I shall pass over the vaudevillian and macabre details that marked the end of this mythomaniacal odyssey!

The interest of this case is not so much in the adventure itself as in what it tells us about the psychology of Miss X's personality. Her whole childhood had been spent in a familial climate that predisposed her to mythomania. Raised between two divorced parents, she dreamed of an ideal home she never knew in reality and realized more keenly with each passing year she would never know. Overshadowed by a sister whom her mother preferred and her father spoiled, she always felt inferior and frustrated. She was jealous of her younger colleagues' marriages as she had been jealous of her younger sister.

Basically this apparently comic history is tragic. When Miss X decided upon the death of her imaginary husband she decided at the same time to deal a death-blow to her dream and illusions.

We have said that all forms of lying are conditioned by a relationship to another. Mythomania is a tendency to satisfy a personal instinct, but even more it is an effort to affirm oneself before others through morbid exhibitionism. The mythomaniac craves an audience; the latter is far more important than the fabricated stories. Indeed, if the mythomaniac could relate authentic stories this would in most cases satisfy his need. Material profit is not necessarily basic to mythomania, although it is usually a factor.

Here is another case from my files.

Paul is sixteen years old. He is a student in a technical school. He is tall and tanned and looks older than he is. In fact, he tries to look older. He rarely associates with his classmates, whom he regards as mere kids. He is not stupid, far from it, but he does poorly in his studies because his mind is always elsewhere. His father died when he was young and his mother remarried. His stepfather is rather passive and lets his wife deal with Paul. He clearly dominates his mother. She for her part covers for him. She never mentions his many failings: lies, theft, failure in school, truancy, etc. Paul likes to be the center of attention. He was a leader among the young people of his parish until a series of thefts sullied his reputation. He is interested in politics and never rides the subway without a copy of a leading political journal, usually the same issue. He gives the impression of being serious. A pair of dark-rimmed glasses, despite their uselessness, reinforces this impression. Paul joined a group of ham radio operators and became friends with a forty-year-old engineer. This friendship flatters him, and he dramatizes his life to his new companion. He explains that he is still in school (four or five years after he should be) because during the war his mother was forced to hide from the Germans in the country. He explains that his father, who in fact died of tuberculosis brought on by the privations of the Occupation, was executed by the Germans. His engineer friend tells Paul about an excellent American station that could be heard in France with special equipment.

A few days later Paul tells his friend that he can obtain the radio for a large sum of money, although considerably less than its actual worth. His friend listens to Paul's convincing arguments. His mother, he explains, works in the American embassy and is the mistress of an American officer. He explains that he discovered the liaison and to buy his silence his mother and her lover will refuse him nothing. The American officer works in communications and for a stipulated sum can have the radio imported to France through the embassy. The balance would then be paid upon delivery. The engineer provides a substantial down payment, and Paul is well launched on his mythomaniacal journey. He is constantly forced to fabricate fresh lies: the American officer is recalled to the States, but he will certainly return with the radio; his tardiness in returning calls forth new explanations; then Paul's mother falls ill. The engineer grows impatient and threatens Paul. One day he demands his investment back. Paul calmly announces that there is no need for concern. He has just heard that the officer has returned with the radio. All they have to do now is pay the balance and it will be delivered forthwith. His mother, he explains, got better and returned to the embassy to work. There she found a letter from her lover saying that he would return in a few days bringing "what he had promised Paul." The engineer immediately apologized, saying he had never doubted his friend's honesty. They converse for some time and Paul gets carried away with a story about a trip he is going to take in the country with his mother and stepfather, pointing out that he would like to have a camera to take some pictures. The engineer offers to lend him his. The camera was Paul's downfall for no sooner had he left his friend than he tried to sell it in a pawnshop. The dealer was suspicious of the young vendor and made a quiet investigation. The affair would have wound up in a court of justice had not Paul's stepfather reimbursed the engineer.

Mythomania and fraudulence often go hand in hand, but it is clear that Paul was more interested in playing a role than in pocketing the money. A later investigation showed that he used most of the money impressing his friends with gifts and lavish entertainment. In other words, the money enabled him to show off. He explained his sudden wealth with a fanciful story about how an industrialist had handsomely rewarded him for signal services rendered.

Vanity is the most important element in mythomania. Very often it is the only explanatory factor. We have already noted this in discussing the intentionality of nonpathological lying. In pathological lying this element is even more prominent. We can scarcely speak of mythomania with respect to the fibs of children and adolescents. "My father has the fastest car in the world." "My mother has a diamond *that big!*" "My brother single-handedly took fifty prisoners during the war." And so forth.

But vanity that is humorous in the young becomes much more serious when it persists in the adult and begins to take on the characteristics of mythomania. One of my patients was famous for his heroism during the war. But an inquiry to verify his exploits soon revealed the vanity of a mythomaniac. On ground, sea, and in the air he had performed extraordinary feats! One day his wife was congratulated for her husband's bravery as a pilot. She expressed surprise and said that her husband had never been in an airplane. He could not bear mediocrity. Even his illness had to be exceptional. He never felt he was being taken seriously enough. One morning I received a curious phone call. "I am X's father. I understand you are treating him and I would like to know what you think of his case. You realize, of course, that he is seriously ill. The doctors have no doubt told you that his is an extraordinary case. I am coming to see him because his mother and I are very upset." I answered that I could not give information over the telephone but would be happy to see him in private. The next day I saw my patient's wife and told her about the strange phone call. She broke out in laughter, for she knew her husband only too well. "His father is miles from here and doesn't even know that he is seeing a doctor." When I saw my patient a few days later I joked about his little game. But nothing jarred him. He had an explanation for everything.

From a psychoanalytic point of view it is customary to link such vanity with certain sexual impulses. This is an illuminating approach, although great care must be taken not to exaggerate. It is all too easy to find sexual motivations for anything at all. But it is perfectly clear

that behind the vanity of mythomania often can be
found the need to affirm a repressed sexuality. It is
even more clear that much mythomania has a sexual
basis. This is equally true of men and women. The
attempt upon one's chastity is, of all themes, the one
that lends itself most readily to fabrication. The mystery of the sexual fact, the lewd interest it arouses, the
way in which it accommodates the double mechanism
of seduction and aggression—all of this offers to the
imagination a theme that everyone can manipulate to
suit himself. The truth of sexual incidents invoked by
the mythomaniac is not *a priori* excluded, although he
may be somewhat perverted and exaggerate a real incident in order to play at once the hero, the victim, and
the accuser. The mythomania of the pervert is the most
dangerous of all, because it carries to their logical conclusion consequences that are willed and foreseen from
the beginning. As P. F. Girard remarks in the volume
already referred to, the perverted and intelligent
mythomaniac is skilled in finding victims among the
mentally retarded and alcoholics. On the other hand,
"perverted mythomaniacs are contagious individuals
from the moral point of view. With their fluency of
speech and imaginative tales they can be both persuasive and seductive. Few are more capable of winning
a following and putting forth a good image. Many
leaders, even among children, find in their mythomaniacal tendencies their principal instrument of re-
cruitment."

It is customary to distinguish between intelligent and
feebleminded mythomaniacs. The seriously handicapped are irresponsible and therefore incapable of
lying, since the latter is an act of intelligence. The less
seriously handicapped can lie a good deal but lie badly.
Mythomania demands an even greater intellectual
effort than does lying. The fabrication of the feeble-

minded deceives few; it usually loses itself in a mythic
construction that bears little resemblance to the habitual mythomaniac's skill. I once knew of a Mongo-
loid who invented a brother. He knew very well that
this was a pure fabrication, yet he acted as though it
were a fact. No hallucination is involved here; merely a
stereotyped construction that is demanding but very
impoverished.

THE MADAME BOVARY COMPLEX

Mythomania sometimes undergoes a transformation.
It then consists less in seeking to play a role than in
really putting oneself in another's shoes. Jules de
Gaultier has coined the expression "the Madame
Bovary complex" to designate "the power a man has to
conceive of himself other than he is." Are we still in
the pathological world or already confronted with a
subnormal aspect of lying?

In reality there are many degrees. Madame Bovary
was somewhat neurotic; but Don Quixote was more so,
as P. F. Girard points out.[2] The forms of lying that
fall under the Bovary complex range all the way from
innocent play to fabrication that approaches madness.
This points to the difficult problem of identity. In play
we always identify, whether with Robinson Crusoe,
Al Capone, or some famous military figure. Education
would be impossible without such a process and all
educators know this perfectly well from their experience. The impossibility for the child to find in his
parents an object of desirable identification is always
unfortunate. In addition to good identifications, which
enable the personality to amplify and individualize itself, to progress toward autonomy and liberation, there

[2] *Ibid.*, p. 115.

are bad identifications, which impede the development of the personality and imprison it in the mold of a prefabricated character. We shall say more about this when we discuss fiction and the imaginary [Chap. 8].

Unable to be himself, the person afflicted with the Madame Bovary complex assumes the personality of another and thus camouflages what he really is. He lies to others by more or less consciously substituting an image for what really is. But we must be careful not to exaggerate the pathological implications of this complex. Jules de Gaultier tried to construct a whole philosophical system on the basis of the Madame Bovary complex considered as "an essential condition of phenomenal life" and thus free of all pathological contamination. The whole last part of his book (which makes the fictive and irrational the basis of the real and the reasonable) turns on a paradox. De Gaultier somewhat abusively proclaims that in all men there is an "irremediable Bovary complex, which makes of error and lying a law of nature, a sickness of the imagination and the mind that obliges man to despise all reality in favor of the unreal." We agree with him, however, when he says that snobbery characterizes the Bovary complex. For what is snobbery but deceitful behavior in which the afflicted find it much more important to conform to a prototype than to themselves? We could have raised the question of snobbery in our discussion of sincerity. For it is a kind of absence of sincerity. One pretends to abide by an ethical code but really does not. Snobbery is contradictory. At times it is a kind of esoteric conformity that ends in a conformity to nonconformity; at other times it takes the form of a British stoicism, which considers it the highest form of sophistication to give the appearance of complete indifference. In all cases the essence of snobbery consists in merging with a physical or psychic uniformity to conceal what one really is. The snob is nothing less than a schemer who is interested in giving others a false opinion of himself in order to exploit them.

Snobbery is compounded of lying and bad faith. One desires primarily to be what is opportune to be in order to achieve certain specified goals rather than be one-self. One lies to others about who one really is and to oneself because the principal objective is to conform to a collective type rather than be authentic.

Obvious forms of snobbery are to be found in dandies, the followers of esoteric schools, surrealists and the like. Less obvious but equally real forms can be found in those who are primarily concerned with impressing others with their social status.

Jules de Gaultier writes: "While snobbery is a super-ficial manifestation of it and is at all times dependent upon it, on the whole snobbery is a triumphant Bovary complex; it is the totality of means used to conceal one's true personality and thus always to appear as a more desirable person than one is."

Are we still in the world? The core of truth is no longer apparent. Only the truth of a function subsists, not the truth of an existence. *Un Grand personnage*,[3] a long novel by Pierre Bost, illustrates the lie of unreality that characterizes those who conceal their true being behind important-sounding titles and social rank.

THE HYSTERICAL LIE

Before discussing the basic problem of hysterical lying, we must first understand what is meant by the term. Without entering into a detailed classification of mental diseases, we offer the following clarifications.

[3] Pierre Bost, *Un Grand personnage*, N.R.F.

There are two schools of thought on this matter. One holds that hysteria and simulation belong to the same nosological category. The other maintains that they are antipodal. By introducing the notion of the unconscious, psychoanalysis has done much to resolve the problem. Hysteria is an unconscious simulation. This raises the question of whether or not we can call it a lie, since lying supposes that the liar is conscious. A true lie implies responsibility, whereas hysterical behavior does not, because it is not consciously willed.

The hysterical person believes in his sickness; he has a kind of faith in it. He who simulates knows that he is intentionally deceiving others. What complicates this issue is that at first sight the hysterical person seems to be conscious of acting out a comic role and deceiving the world.

Two examples will illustrate this point. While I was an intern I knew a patient who could not walk, although there was no manifest physical reason for this. He had been wounded in the war and wanted to receive the disability pension a bed-ridden condition would have given him a right to. From all evidence his pseudoparalytic attitude was conscious and voluntary. None of the classic symptoms of paralysis could be observed in him; nor were any of the symptoms of hysterical paralysis observable. He was a poor liar and it soon turned out that he was deliberately pretending.

Here is a quite different case. Helen, a young girl of nine, was brought to me because of a limp. None of my medical colleagues could find any organic cause for her infirmity. The examination was totally negative. The child walked with a wide sweeping movement like a hemiplegic. What did we learn from her family? For some time her grandmother, who was still a relatively young sixty, had been afflicted with hemiplegia. The little girl had been spoiled by her grandmother. Fur-

thermore, the latter was unable to do much housework.
Helen was obliged to cook, set the table, and do the
dishes. The family's attention was centered on the ail-
ing grandmother and less and less heed was paid to
her. Helen sincerely suffered from her grandmother's
illness and was also sincerely embarrassed by her difficulty in walking. She could no longer go to school,
where she was an excellent student, or go downstairs to
play with her friends. Her hysteria seemed deliberate,
but in fact her will had nothing to do with it. She
unconsciously assumed the behavior of a paralytic as a
way of identifying with a beloved grandmother. The
difference between hysteria and simulation is often difficult to make clear to those who have not gone beyond
a merely clinical observation of the facts.

A hysterical state can last indefinitely, long after its
utilitarian value has ended. Thus it differs from the
fabrication of the mythomaniac, which lasts only as
long as it is useful.

Even a serious danger does not always cure hysteria.
One of my teachers often cited the case of a hemiplegia
paralytic who fell in the river on a fishing trip and
nearly drowned because, although a very good swim-
mer, he could swim only with the one arm and leg not
affected by his hysteria. The same teacher also told his
students that when he wanted to furnish proof of a
hysterical paralysis that others considered merely simu-
lated he exploded a huge firecracker under the patient's
bed. The patient did not move, even after the bed-
clothes had caught fire, and had to be helped to safety
by those in attendance.

The hysterical person cannot be considered a liar,
since he does not know that he lies; but, as we have
indicated, hysteria can foster lying and mythomania.

It is in fact impossible to strictly classify the forms
of pathological lying, especially in children. Quoting

Professor Heuyer, Sutter says: "In child psychiatry classifications are merely dialectical expedients. . . . In this domain, there is nothing static; everything is dominated by the dynamic notion of evolution."

That is why we must not be surprised to find several varieties of the lying mentality in the same subject, depending on the kind of sickness that motivates it.

Some circumstances can almost completely suppress a drive that no longer finds it expedient to manifest itself, while other circumstances cause what are only germinal drives to develop. Thus the case of Jean Cocteau's *Thomas the Impostor.* A confusion in identity makes him suddenly consider himself the son of a famous general. The web of deceit weaves itself spontaneously until Thomas is caught up in a fiction that eventually kills him.

THE NEUROTIC LIE

Mythomania, the Bovary complex, and hysteria are in themselves neurotic lies; but there are still others. If mythomania represents the sickness of lying we can say with Sutter that there the neurotic lie can nonetheless be distinguished from it. We are not concerned with describing how lying manifests itself in the different forms of neurosis but rather with studying the morbid character it takes on as a result of the encounter of certain temperaments with certain circumstances.

Such lies differ from mythomania in the sense that they normally do not stem from an innate drive nor vain exhibitionism. Quite often the contrary is the case. The mythomaniac lies to call attention to himself; others lie to remain unnoticed. The mythomaniac builds a fictional pyramid and climbs on top of it; others inevitably slide down the slopes toward the shadowy base.

Here is an example. John is eleven years old. He is of average intelligence and an average student. He is timid and fears his teacher. Nor is he at ease with his parents, although they are not unduly strict. One evening dinner is served late because guests are invited. John goes to bed without doing his homework. The next morning he is uneasy and worries about being questioned in class. He goes to school with a heavy heart. But he cannot go in. He notices in the distance the last of his classmates entering. Then the bell rings and the school doors close. John roams the streets all morning. He wonders what he will tell his parents at noon. And how will he explain his absence to his teacher? Would his mother fabricate an excuse? When he goes home to lunch he dares not confess his truancy. This would displease his father. He pretends to be in a good mood at table and recounts an incident that happened in class that morning as evidence that he had been to school. He also said: "I was lucky. I wasn't questioned." That afternoon he played the truant again. It began to rain, and John spent the afternoon riding around the city in the subway. The crowds, the kaleidoscope of lighted stations, and the dark tunnels benumbed his mind. He did not know what he would do when he went home that night. As soon as he came in he took out his books and began to do imaginary homework. The same thing happened on Saturday.

On Monday report cards were due. Wouldn't some explanation for his two-day absence be called for? The mail usually arrived before he left for school. He intercepted the postman and at noon when his parents expressed surprise at not receiving his report card, John said: "Nothing to worry about. Our teacher is sick and a replacement has taken over his classes." This state of affairs continued for about a week. One day a school official arrived to investigate John's prolonged absence, and John was exposed.

John was not a mythomaniac. He did not lie for the sake of lying, but solely because he dared not take the risk of being questioned on material he had not prepared.

We encounter cases of this sort daily, not only among children but equally among adults who have no desire to lie but do so out of fear of affirming who they are or what they are doing.

One of my patients was a student. He was not basically a liar, but each time exams came around he found himself in an impossible position. For the years I knew him the same thing always happened. Alone in Paris (his rather wealthy parents lived in their country estate) he pursued a number of unrelated courses. If he failed an exam he could never bring himself to admit it to his parents. If, on the other hand, he was successful, his satisfaction compensated for paternal reprobation and he would admit to a previous failure. Thus the time gained by admitted failures compensated for the time lost by false successes, and he succeeded in establishing a temporary balance. He was never in the year of school his parents supposed him to be. Thus he was continually forced to lie. I might note that I was treating this young man for a serious case of masochism. To what extend did his lying nourish this affliction?

Another of my patients could not be classified as a mythomaniac. He was in many ways the most open and loyal of men, but there were certain situations he could not confront. As a child he was not unlike John, described above. Fear of failure caused him to seek escape in a mountain of lies. Since he was very intelligent he easily passed his examinations and eventually became a lawyer.

He joined an important firm, but the hierarchical structure of the latter reminded him of his college days when he was always afraid of being exposed. One day he forgot a brief that his employer had particularly asked for. To admit this would have brought about no serious consequences; certainly his career would not have been jeopardized in any way. But out of fear he disappeared for several days, spending his mornings in bed and afternoons and evenings in theaters and bars. He offered no explanation to his firm and the first letter from his employer went unanswered. He later informed him that he was ill. The reason for his absence was finally discovered, but, since he was a valuable man, he was forgiven. Two or three years later, he wanted to marry a divorced woman, but he could not bring himself to tell his parents. He fled to a secluded country retreat with his lady-love. He wired his employer that his father had fallen seriously ill while traveling abroad. He invented another excuse for his family and convinced his young love that because of threats against his life it was mandatory for them to stay out of circulation for a time.

Because of his professional competence he was once again forgiven. He also made up with his parents. Then one day he was sent on a business trip abroad. His wife remained behind with their infant twins. While abroad he fell in love with the wife of the local manager of the firm he represented. He convinced her that he was the most miserable of creatures, and she soon became his chief consolation. The woman's husband suspected what was going on and alerted the head office. Things took a turn for the worse. Our hero again disappeared for several weeks, after having informed his wife that business would detain him abroad indefinitely. But this time he irretrievably endangered his career and family.

This man could not face reality. He had a gift for getting into impossible predicaments without being able to face the consequences.

In reality he suffered from a fear of impotency and never thought he would be up to the situation. This accounts for his frequent flights from reality and lying. What was the origin of this impotency complex? As a youth he had undergone an operation on his testicles. An older companion told him that he could never marry or father children. Although later events proved this false, it left him with an inferiority complex. He could never tolerate being seen in the nude, either literally or figuratively.

These examples show that many neurotic lies can be considered pathological. But the fact that they are pathological does not absolve the liar from all responsibility. Neurosis can explain the why of lying and the liar's attitude toward reality; it can even diminish responsibility. But it can never suppress it entirely. Only a totally alienated person lacks the freedom that is an indispensable condition of lying. Nothing is more dangerous than those theories that are always ready to eliminate responsibility because of a pathological condition. A sick person is not automatically irresponsible and to absolve him of the responsibility he is still capable of would rish making his state worse. What often happens with a mental patient is a displacement of his sense of responsibility. This makes him exaggerate insignificant details and overlook the substantial. This is the case, for example, with the scrupulous. A neuropsychiatrist could make two mistakes with respect to a liar. He could absolve him of all moral responsibility or he could deny the existence of the moral dimension altogether. The psychotherapist's work with liars usually consists of the following: removing the false sense of responsibility that compels them to lie and, secondly, pointing out the areas where it is still possible to make a responsible effort. I favor a psychotherapy of analytic inspiration over integral psychoanalysis. It is more flexible and as a result the only one that can be habitually used in treating children.

We saw earlier that lying is as a rule one of the child's minor offenses. My experience has shown that it is often associated with delinquent acts, theft in particular. Lying is rarely an isolated act. Pure mythomania that is neither utilitarian nor perverse is rarely found. Neurotic lying is almost always related to other morbid symptoms and behavioral aberrations. Theft, escape, refusal to do schoolwork, and some sadomasochistic tendencies are most frequently associated with lying. Lying is the servant of other abnormal drives. Any analysis that is limited to the fact of lying would be superficial, because we must as a rule seek out the motivation of neurotic troubles other than lying itself. The root motivation of lying is often uniquely the desire to conceal one's other neurotic drives.

REVERIE

Is it normal to include reverie among pathological lies? Where does normal reverie stop? Is it to be defined as the fantasy that is a part of everyone's life? The free play of ideas? Or a fixation on this or that subject that pleases us? We are all to some extent mythomaniacs in our dreams. Who has not dreamed that he accomplished great feats or, on the other hand, suffered the most unhappy of fates? Who has not done in his dreams what he would never dare in real life?

How many have been Don Juans in their dreams,
whereas in real life their love lives are as dull as ditch-
water? None of this is in the least pathological, but
certain forms of reverie constitute a veritable derange-
ment of the imagination. Can one say that the dreamer
lies to himself? No, because he does not intend to
deceive anyone. Yet he is taken in by his own dream.
Though he does not deceive himself, his greatest desire
is nonetheless (even though he does not admit it) to
lose contact with reality in order to live in the truth of
dreamland and thus deceive himself in the end. Dreaming is in some sense the pursuit of a lie we can never
completely believe. It is a mechanism of compensation.
In dreams we are everything we are not and cannot be
in reality. Some children are perpetually in a dreamlike
state. Sartre puts this well in *The Words*, writing about
his childhood, which was unusually deprived of contact
with others. His life was filled with fantasies that he
desperately hoped were true. Many dream for the sake
of dreaming and nothing else; they think something is
wrong when reality takes the place of their dreams.
Others find more satisfaction in imaginative anticipation than in realization. Contact with reality always
constricts the senses and emotions by limiting them to
what is effectively perceived. In reality we cannot
manipulate facts to suit our fancy (except in retrospect). In this sense Flaubert could write: "Reading
moves me more than a real misfortune." We are not
far here from the Bovary complex already spoken of.
Demonstrating the role of the imagination in Madame
Bovary's psychology, Jules de Gaultier writes: "Nothing but images influences her, nothing but what was
previously deformed and adopted to her own desires by
pure imagination." One of my patients lived almost
constantly in a fantasy world and told me that he
found it more pleasurable to dream of certain foods

than to eat them in reality, because for him material truth always sullied the absolute vision of his imagination. But he dreamed far more of erotic matters, accompanied by solitary acts, than of food. Can this be classified a lie? Whatever the answer, it is clear that such fantasies belong more to the domain of fiction than truth.

I have known sick people who over a period of years awaited impatiently for evening to come so they could in obscurity and silence return to writing an endless novel, taking up each time where they had left off the evening before. They were not children but adults seeking escape by seeing themselves other than they were in fiction where the same themes daily took on new meanings. One of my patients, whom we shall call Olivier, entitled his novel *Poor Olivier*. Each day a new episode was required to provide him with the masochistic ration he found necessary to feed his self-pity. I have known others for whom the culminating periods of their dreams were the rewards that they accorded themselves at minutely calculated intervals. For some, dreaming becomes confounded with a kind of pious meditation in which they think they are in the presence of the infinite and absolute. But in fact they imagined the infinite or absolute in the autism of their schizophrenia.

Should reverie be prohibited because it leads to unreality and lying? Certainly not. Just as the indentification that risks leading to a neurotic Bovary complex can serve the development of the personality, so too, in the fog of an uncontrolled reverie we can discover a little of our own truth.

We could cite whole pages of Sartre's *The Words*[4] to show the magic of reverie, which seeks in immediate

[4] J.-P. Sartre, *The Words*, trans. Bernard Frechtman, George Braziller, New York, 1964.

reality what can be transmuted imaginatively and ig-
nores everything else.

I would slip into the study; it was already dark there; two
candles were burning on the piano. The semi-darkness served
my purpose. I would seize my grandfather's ruler; it was my
rapier; his paper-cutter was my dagger; I became then and
there the flat image of a musketeer. Sometimes I had to wait
for inspiration: to gain time, I the illustrious swashbuckler
would decide that an important matter obliged me to
remain incognito. I had to receive blows without hitting back
and to display my courage by feigning cowardice. I would
walk around the room, my eyes glowering, my head bowed,
shuffling my feet. I would indicate by a sudden start from
time to time that I had been slapped or kicked in the behind,
but I was careful not to react; I made a mental note of my
insulter's name. Finally, the music, of which I had taken a
huge dose, began to act. The piano forced its rhythm on me
like a voodoo drum. The *Fantasia Impromptu* substituted for
my soul; it inhabited me, gave me an unknown past, a blaz-
ing and mortal future. I was possessed, the demon had
seized me and was shaking me like a plum tree. To horse!
I was mare and rider, bestrider and bestridden. I dashed
over hill and dale, from the door to the window. I spy the
duke, I dismount, I inform him by silent movements of my
lips that I consider him illegitimate. He unleashes his hench-
men. My whirling sword is a bulwark of steel. From time
to time, I run someone through. Immediately I about-face,
I become the stabbed ruffian, I fall, I die on the carpet. Then
I secretly withdraw from the corpse, I stand up again, I go
back to my role of knight-errant. I played all the characters:
as knight, I slapped the duke; I spun about; as duke, I received the slap. But I did not embody the wicked for long,
because I was always impatient to return to the major role,
to myself. Invincible, I triumphed over all. But, as in my
nocturnal narratives, I put off my triumph indefinitely because I was afraid of the depression that would follow.

I'm defending a young countess against the King's own
brother. What slaughter! But my mother has turned the

page; the allegro gives way to a tender adagio; I finish off the carnage in quick time, I smile at the lady. She loves me; the music says so. And I love her too, perhaps. My heart slowly fills with love. What does one do when one is in love? I take her arm, we stroll in the meadow. There must be more to it than that. Summoned in haste, the bandits and the duke's men help me out. They attack us, a hundred against one. I kill ninety of them, the other ten kidnap the countess.

This is the moment to look into my dismal years. The woman who loves me is held captive. The whole police force of the kingdom is after me. I'm an outlaw who's being hunted down, a poor unhappy wretch. All I have left is my conscience and my sword. I would pace the study with a woe-begone look. Chopin's passionate sadness would gradually fill me. Sometimes I would skim through my life, I would skip two or three years to assure myself that all would end well, that the King would restore my titles, my lands, and a fiancée almost intact and that he would ask my forgiveness. But I would immediately jump back to my unhappy situation of two or three years earlier. That moment charmed me; fiction merged with truth. As a heartsore vagabond seeking justice, I resembled, like a twin brother, the child who was at loose ends, a burden to himself, in search of a reason for living, who prowled about, to a musical accompaniment, in his grandfather's study. Without dropping the role, I took advantage of the resemblance to amalgamate our destinies; reassured as to the final victory, I would regard my tribulations as the surest way to achieve it. I would see through my abjection to the future glory that was its true cause. Schumann's sonata would finally convince me: I was both the creature who despairs and the God who has always saved him since the beginning of time. What a joy to be able to be bursting with affliction; I had a right to be on the outs with the universe. Weary of easy successes, I relished the delights of melancholy, the pungent pleasure of resentment. An object of the tenderest care, petted and coddled, without desires. I rushed headlong into an imaginary destitution. Eight years of felicity had ended only in giving me a taste for martyrdom. Instead of my usual judges, who were all predisposed in my favor, I set up a surly court that was ready to condemn me without a hearing. I wrested an acquittal from it, congratulations, a just retribution. I had read the story of Griselda a dozen times with a thrill of pleasure. Yet I did not like to suffer, and my early desires were cruel: The defender of so many princesses had no scruples about mentally spanking the little girl next door. What pleased me about that not very praiseworthy story was the victim's sadism and the inflexible virtue that ended with the fiendish husband on his knees. That was what I wanted for myself: to force the magistrates to kneel, to make them revere me so as to punish them for their bias. But I kept putting off the acquittal to the following day. I remained a future hero and longed for a consecration that I continually postponed.

I think that this double melancholy, which I actually felt and at which I played, was an expression of my disappointment. All my exploits, laid end to end, were only a string of random events. When my mother struck the final chords of the *Fantasia Impromptu*, I fell back into the memoryless time of fatherless orphans, of orphanless knights-errant. Whether as a hero or schoolboy, doing the same dictations, the same doughty deeds, over and over, I remained locked up in the prison of repetition.[5]

Later Sartre's reverie transports him to the highest ecstasy. But regretfully he retained some lucidity while fearing that he would lose it.

Faith, even when profound, is never entire. One must constantly prop it up, or at least refrain from ruining it. I was consecrated, illustrious. I had my tomb in Père Lachaise Cemetery and perhaps in the Pantheon; an avenue was named after me in Paris, as were public squares in the provinces and in foreign countries. Yet, at the core of my optimism I had a sneaking feeling that I lacked substance. At Saint Anne's Psychiatric Clinic, a patient cried out in bed: "I'm a prince! Arrest the Grand Duke!" Someone went up to him and whispered in his ear: "Blow your nose!" and

[5] *Ibid.*, pp. 125 ff.

he blew his nose. He was asked: "What's your occupation?"
He answered quietly: "Shoemaker," and started shouting
again. I imagine that we're all like that man. In any case,
at the beginning of my ninth year, I resembled him: I was
a prince and a shoemaker.

Two years later, I would have been considered cured. The
prince had disappeared, the shoemaker believed in nothing,
I had even stopped writing. The "novel notebooks" had been
thrown out, mislaid, or burned and had made way for gram-
mar, arithmetic, and dictation notebooks. If someone had
crept into my head, which was open to all the winds, he
would have come upon a few busts, a stray multiplication
table and the rule of three, thirty-two counties with the
chief town of each but not the sub-prefecture, a rose called
rosarosarosamrosaerosaerosa, some historical and literary
monuments, a few polite maxims engraved on stiles, and
sometimes, like a scarf of mist hovering over this sad garden,
a sadistic reverie. Not a single female orphan. No sign of a
gallant knight. The words hero, martyr, and saint were not
inscribed anywhere, not repeated by any voice. The ex-
Pardaillan received satisfactory health reports every term:
child of average intelligence, very well behaved, not gifted
for the exact sciences, imaginative but not excessively, sensitive; quite normal, despite a certain affectedness which,
moreover, was on the wane. But I had gone completely mad.[6]

Reverie is the imaginary that is lived. It is perhaps
the door to madness and hell; but it is also the gateway
to poetry and authenticity.

Is it possible or even desirable to protect oneself
from fiction and reverie? Could one be fully oneself
without the imaginary and fiction, which are the
sources of eternally true myths, of imperishable masterpieces, as well as the greatest discoveries?

Reverie constitutes a dialogue between the conscious
self and the deeper layers of the self that border on
the world of the instincts. Moreover, in analysis a

[6] *Ibid.*, pp. 208–209.

patient's free association is frequently much more revealing when it rambles into the world of the imagination. When a patient warns the analyst that he is going to fabricate and invent he is often most himself and most susceptible to the healing art of therapy.

6

Fidelity

THE PROBLEMS posed by the virtue of fidelity are directly related to the problems of lying, loyalty, and sincerity. But we must not limit fidelity to its co-ordinates with lying and bad faith. Fidelity is more related to the question of truth. Urs von Balthasar, in his book on the phenomenology of truth, insists on the profound meaning of the Hebrew word for truth: *Ehmet*. This word not only means truth but, also more deeply, fidelity and trust. The identity of the same Hebrew word for truth and fidelity is particularly significant. Yahweh is the God of truth as well as of fidelity. We can trust in him because he is fidelity; we must trust in him because he is truth.

At the end of an earlier chapter, we intimated that fidelity could lead to a conflict between loyalty and sincerity.

Not to be faithful is to deceive another on the value of a commitment; to be faithful is sometimes to risk not being sincere with oneself out of loyalty. Fidelity can be a stumbling block to both loyalty and sincerity. In a superficial way, it can become an impasse with lying the only exit. Fidelity can be called into question from many different and even contradictory points of view. To what extent does an infraction of fidelity imply or not imply an element of lying? To renounce one's commitments is deliberately to deceive, to lie in a cynical fashion by rejecting what had until then been considered an obligation. It would perhaps be more exact to say that infidelity is an *a posteriori* proof that a previous commitment has been betrayed. By infidelity man lies to another and discovers that he himself is a liar. It is easy to see how fidelity can be exercised in many different ways: fidelity to a business contract that is duly notarized or merely agreed to verbally; fidelity to a religious or political conviction; fidelity to a state of life. To deceive one's partner is to lie, to hide the truth, to betray one's commitment, to lie a lie.

An offense against fidelity is much more than a simple lie. More than any act of lying it is an act of exteriority toward another. In simply lying only the communication of the truth to another who is entitled to it is affected. There is a prior commitment in fidelity that is always more or less bound to a sworn faith; to fail in fidelity is always more or less a perjury.

In lying the quality and rights of the person lied to alter the responsibility involved; in fidelity, on the other hand, the sworn faith is integrally due. The pact exists in itself. It cannot be declared null by the sole will of one of the parties or even, in some cases, both parties. Marriage, made indissoluble by the sacramental seal, would be an example.

Jankelevitch quite correctly begins his study of the virtues with fidelity. The chapter is entitled "Courage and Fidelity." Fidelity is the heroic permanence of sworn faith. This does not mean that one must always be heroic in order to be faithful; but there can be no fidelity that does not imply courage and eventually sacrifice. Fidelity is not the same as sincerity, loyalty, or good faith. Either it is or it is not. Why then speak of it in a discussion of lying? Because in every failure of fidelity there is necessarily a lie to someone or to something. It might be objected that blatant disregard of one's commitments deceives no one and that there is therefore no intention of lying. Consider, for example, the facts and language by which such disregard is expressed. We say that so and so deceives his wife, whether the latter knows it or not. When she learns the truth, a woman always considers herself deceived.

We have distinguished the "liar" and "the person lied to." Both are involved in infidelity. The lie could have begun with the commitment we took, either flagrantly in the sense that we knew we would not keep it or in the sense that we were already in a state of bad faith, which supposes the possibility of infidelity. But in most cases lying and bad faith do not emerge until after we have committed ourselves in fidelity.

Lying pertains to the domain of the transcendent; infidelity pertains to the domain of the contingent and singular. The liar denies something external that exists independently of himself; the unfaithful person denies something that is personal to him, that he created out of whole cloth and accepted in relationship to another.

The truth that engages loyalty needs no seal. *It is.* But fidelity almost always calls for a seal, something to make it official as it were: one's word, a signed contract, even a sacrament. Truth is independent of being; fidelity is being itself. Gabriel Marcel has written that being is the place of fidelity. We may also say that "the power to be faithful" is one of the constituent elements of being that authenticates and extends it. The power to commit oneself for the future and the fact of feeling oneself bound by fidelity to the past assures the temporal continuity of being.

To be unfaithful is to lie to one to whom one has sworn fidelity; but it is also to lie to oneself in the commitment one has taken. Infidelity brings about bad faith more than does lying. We put ourselves in a state of bad faith more to excuse our infidelity than for any other reason. Fidelity is permanence; it is courage over a long period of time rather than for the moment. Fidelity can only fully exist if it is proven. We are never truly faithful except insofar as we are so *despite* something or someone or at least are disposed to overcome obstacles. One is faithful for better or worse. Loyalty and sincerity can suffer failure and eclipses. Intermittent fidelity is no longer fidelity. For this reason fidelity is distinct from lying and bad faith. Jankelevitch writes: "Since the law of time is perpetual alterity we must choose between fidelity and sincerity: imperturbable coherence at the expense of sincerity (which always makes us contemporaneous with ourselves) or sincerity at the price of contradiction and ingratitude. . . . The intention of sincerity joins with the straight line of fidelity to form a more or less open angle. The degree of this angle indicates the degree of hypocrisy that the faithful person, out of superstitious attachment to the letter of his promise, permits to come between his truth and his oath. The faithful person is always behind himself." Fidelity is the concordance between what is, what will be, and what has been.

Fidelity raises numerous difficulties because of the possibility of certain variations in sincerity. Is it always perjury to renounce one unconditional fidelity? Does not the discovery of one's error sometimes justify abjuration, which is not necessarily identical with perjury? Does the fact of abjuring what we promised without sufficient thought expose us to living a continual lie? Are not some forms of fidelity more like defiance in maintaining unconditional attachment to what is evidently inconsistent and without substance? This seems to be what Nietzsche meant when he wrote in *The Gay Science:* "It is out of pure defiance that he holds to a cause that he no longer believes in—but he calls it fidelity."

Will not abjuration gradually justify itself by the progressive encroachment of a state of bad faith? It is here that the perspective of infidelity becomes part of the complexity of lying and bad faith. Fidelity that is not called into question falls outside the scope of our considerations, although it is necessarily bound up with patterns of thought and behavior that are sincere and loyal.

It is not our intention here to discuss the eventual legitimacy of abjuring a faith that we have been burdened with since childhood. Nor shall we discuss the question of divorce, which is a clear rejection of a prior oath. But we are concerned with the extent to which we lie in order to live in occult contravention of our commitments and to what extent we put ourselves in a state of bad faith in order to justify the rejection of an oath of fidelity.

In the chapter on bad faith and sincerity we cited the example of a man who gradually justified deserting his family in the name of false sincerity in order to marry his secretary. Such examples could be multiplied endlessly. In my medical practice I encounter problems of fidelity and infidelity every day. The unfaithful men or women will as a rule invent the best of reasons to justify their conduct. They begin with small lies to themselves and thus imperceptibly dispose themselves to the inevitable advent of the unfaithful act. In the name of sincerity, or apparent sincerity, they become unfaithful. They put themselves in a situation where it would be an intolerable lie to remain faithful. Then they lie to the other to prevent discovery of their infidelity and lie increasingly to themselves in order to justify their infidelity. They deceive their spouse, abandoning him or her out of sincerity and thus avoid lying to them. False sincerity becomes the habitual and justifying accompaniment of all betrayals. One lies and deceives in the name of sincerity in order to follow a course of action one confuses with the truth. But it should be remembered that destiny does not exclude duty, and if Antigone's destiny is to bury Polyneices it is also her duty, born of fidelity to commitments superior to those imposed upon her by her father, Creon. Fidelity cannot be taken for granted; it must be worked at. Without falling into a Kantian voluntarism, we may say that one cannot remain faithful without an effort of the will, and we can will only by loving. To take refuge behind the weight of destiny in order to escape the imperatives of fidelity under the pretext of sincerity with oneself is a solution of expedience that blindly accepts all future betrayals, all lies, and all forms of bad faith. It is to accept in advance the possibility of being other than what one **is**. We must beware of that kind of sincerity that seeks justification rather than justice! When sincerity is nothing more than egoism that legitimizes the absence of fidelity to the other, it is a very pathetic sincerity. Love often dies because we neglect to cultivate it. But it is more often killed by lying and bad faith, the worms that gnaw away the substance of fidelity. We have said that fidelity implies heroism. To the extent that fidelity is nourished by the love that forms its basis, a continuing love that protects it against all onslaughts, it will be respected. I confess to a very limited respect for those forms of fidelity that are cloaked in sado-masochistic exhibitionism. Fidelity must be total but humble, simple but sweet. On this question I am far from the position of Paul Claudel. When Claudel says that married couples must sacrifice pleasure to ends outside of themselves I am not convinced. Such forced fidelity can be neither normal, healthy, nor true. But even Claudel cannot recommend pure love. The truth of Prouhèze and Rodrigue is not total renouncement. They are perhaps faithful out of duty. But there is in their relationship a renouncement and a will for the impossible that go beyond fidelity and come much closer to truth.

Although fidelity is the expression of permanence in time, of the constant, the irreversible, and the irrevocable, is it not a static, fixed concept? As truth is what is, but admits of a progressive unfolding, so fidelity that is only an agent of permanence would be a very impoverished fidelity. We are not speaking of fidelity to absolute commitments, such as religious faith, but of fidelity to temporal commitments. This will fall prey to bad faith and lying if, presumptuously, we believe it to be unshakable and definitely acquired once and for all. Many marriages are compromised from the beginning because the couples think they are magically sheltered from lying and bad faith by the mere fact that they have committed themselves. Fidelity must be continually questioned and nourished or it will open the door to bad faith. The best way to be faithful and keep one's good faith is to frequently question the fragility of fidelity, to realize that it is continually threatened and could at any moment flounder. Many unfaithful men and women have told me that they were surprised by the apparent and unforeseen suddenness of their betrayal. Until the fall, it seemed to them that their unconditional fidelity was secure and that nothing could ever dissolve it.

Fidelity is also a bilateral commitment, a contract. It must be renewed daily by contact with the other's thought. Love is strengthened by fidelity, and fidelity exists only by love. "A love that is not faithful is a contradiction as absurd as a square circle. A love that is willing to share its object with others is necessarily insincere. Likewise, a love that admits the future eventuality of its own disaffection is a mere imposture." (Jankelevitch)

On the basis of this remark we might observe that between a marriage that is contracted and willed indissoluble and a marriage that knowingly admits of an eventual dissolution there is a radically different conception of the very notion of marriage.

Fidelity is living only when it is continually growing and being enriched. A fidelity that diminishes and ends in degradation is worth very little. Fidelity must be lucid toward itself. Taken literally it can sometimes become a lie and negation. Lucid infidelity can in exceptional cases become a creative affirmation, but one must constantly be on guard against hubris, that blind pride, which tempts us to bad faith and opens the door to denials. Fidelity that is active, clairvoyant, and persevering, that does not yield to the bad faith of false sincerity and does not flounder under the blows of fate, remains the heroic virtue *par excellence*. As Jankelevitch remarks at the end of his chapter on fidelity, Penelope remained faithful and is the real heroine of the *Odyssey* whereas Ulysses was a trickster and liar. The true theme of the epic is Ulysses' return to his faithful Penelope and not the vicissitudes of his voyage.

Through fidelity the permanence of the self is affirmed. Loyalty has different objects and is not exercised in a continuous fashion. Although one is always obliged to be loyal, one is not constantly obliged to exercise the virtue of loyalty. Likewise, sincerity can be subject to fluctuations that are justified by circumstances. And good faith often implies the obligation to revise one's sincerity toward oneself.

Fidelity in commitment affirms that there is something in me that will endure, that will obligate me, that will bind me. It is both the expression of my liberty and the free acceptance of a certain alienation of my liberty. Lying is the expression of liberty vis-à-vis the truth; infidelity is the expression of a liberty vis-à-vis a binding commitment, which was in itself the consequence of an exercise of liberty. A clear lack of freedom when we commit ourselves is in itself sufficient to liberate us from the obligation of remaining faithful to it. I have no right to commit myself without sufficient liberty. Because I wish to remain faithful, I affirm at the same time the permanence of my person and the permanence of my liberty. Only through lying or bad faith can I escape the imperative of a fidelity promised in all liberty. But here we must point out that what counts in my commitment to fidelity is the consciousness of freedom I had when I made my commitment and not that which may have been accrued later on.[1]

I shall close this chapter by reflecting on two epitaphs. Both men were priests who had renounced their faith. Alfred Loisy wanted to have the following inscribed on his tomb:

[1] Let us recall that in the process of annulling a marriage, what is all important is one's state of freedom at the time the marriage was contracted. Whatever happens afterwards is of no consequence whatsoever.

Alfred Loisy — *priest*

thus signifying that despite his religious evolution he did not renounce his sacerdotal commitment and remained faithful to it even in death, even though he had broken with the organizational church.

Jury wrote: "In the same spirit as Loisy I wish to have written on my tomb:

Paul Jury — *faithful*"

Faithful to what? Solely to himself, he has told us. This is to reject the other. In his proud epitaph he denied that one must be faithful to something or someone. Fidelity that is only fidelity to oneself is not even likely to be sincere.

Fidelity is as a rule more valuable than sincerity, because it is closer to charity. One is sincere for oneself, but one is faithful for others.

Without ceasing to be sincere toward oneself, we can for reasons of fidelity, loyalty, or fraternal charity take certain attitudes and perform certain acts that do not exactly correspond to what one might have wished but that one judges in conscience to be in the best interests of the common good. We have already cited the case of the priest who had lost his faith but continued to minister to his fellow prisoners.

We might also compare the atheist Jean-Paul Sartre's gesture. While a war prisoner he wrote an extraordinary Christmas story called *"Bariona."*[2] This could

---

[2] *"Bariona"* was not published, but the author did permit some mimeographed copies to be circulated, accompanied by a letter that said: "The fact that I drew upon Christian mythology does not mean that the direction of my thinking changed for even a minute during my imprisonment. It was simply a question of finding a theme capable of bringing about the greatest union between Christians and unbelievers on Christmas eve."

hardly have been a theme close to his heart, but without renouncing his own convictions he wanted to be faithful to the spirit of fraternity that united him to his comrades.

7

The Veracity of Testimony
and Confesssion: A Critical Study

WITNESS

THE QUESTION of lying and bad faith leads us to a critical study of testimony.

We are always ready to accuse others of lying. But to what extent are we ourselves liars? When testimony is at issue, whether before a tribunal of justice or in some other circumstance, are we certain of always being able to tell the truth?

There are several categories of false witness: the false witness that is clearly a lie; false witness that results from the fact that we have put ourselves in a state of bad faith and can no longer be objective, especially if an element of passion enters; finally, the false witness of good faith, which is not an intentional lie but simply an unconscious countertruth.

A study of testimony will enable us to see how difficult it is to affirm the truth consciously and objectively. It should make us more indulgent toward those we are prone, rightly or wrongly, to accuse of lying.

In 1950 a meeting of alienists and neurologists was

held at Rennes to discuss the juridical value of testimony. False sentences may be handed down because witnesses, whether voluntarily or not, bore false testimony.

With Michel Cenac we can distinguish three stages in the resolution of the critical problem of testimony. In a first stage we consider that the worth of the testimony is equivalent to the worth of the witness. A witness who is judged normal and trustworthy is considered worthy of being believed because he seems of sound body and mind and enjoys a good reputation. In his *Remembrance of Things Past* Marcel Proust alerts us to the dangers of such criteria. He cites the example of how the testimony of a man of proven morality resulted in the unjust condemnation of two people. This witness was in fact a scoundrel. At the end of the nineteenth and the beginning of the twentieth century the veracity of testimony was subjected to experimental criteria under the influence of psychologists and psychiatrists. More recently what seems to have dominated is the quality of the testimony, the dominant preoccupation being to determine whether a given witness is materially and psychologically better suited than someone else to give testimony about a specific event.

It is a question, on the one hand, of criticizing the materiality of true testimony according to the circumstances. On the other hand, since each witness is evaluated from the point of view of his personal psychological context, it became necessary to seek out the conscious or unconscious influences that may have interfered with his testimony—and this quite apart from the question of bad faith. Suspect testimony may contain something authentic once it is reintegrated into its material and psychological context.

In *Les Témoins,* one of his best novels, Georges

Simenon illustrates the extent to which testimony can be deformed in all good faith by circumstances.

Here is a personal memory. On the morning of February 7, 1934, I met two school companions who had both participated in the events of February 6. Both witnessed the events at close range. They were of two different political persuasions. One was an active member of Action Française; the other was sympathetic to leftist intellectual movements. The testimony of the two was totally different. They largely agreed on how the police acted; but their opinions differed absolutely on the activity of the different political groups that participated in the demonstration. Even on points of detail, such as the hour and the origin of the first outburst of gunfire, they held different opinions. Yet neither of the two could be suspected of bad faith.

I frequently ask myself the following question: Would I be able to offer precise information about something that happened at a certain hour, in a given place? If there is no *a priori* reason why our attention should be attracted by something, if our consciousness is not initially fixed on the facts, then we remember them very incompletely and superficially. If we try to recall them in response to a specific question, our memory is likely to be deformed by the emotional character of the situation.

We remember with relative exactness the new or exceptional. But what is routine and ordinary we remember poorly.

I remember very clearly the small brown moustache, silk scarf, and tie pin of the man with whom I shared my first train ride. I also remember my Pullman companion on a trip during the Occupation when the train derailed inside a tunnel. I remember equally clearly the fat man with froglike features who sat next to me on

my first airplane trip. But how many other traveling
companions have I forgotten completely!

A number of experiments have been conducted on
the value of testimony. We shall rely heavily on Claparède as quoted by Cenac in his report. Claparède, in
his lectures on judiciary psychology in Geneva, used to
ask his students a series of questions concerning places
they frequented daily. For example:

Is there a window on the side of the university build-
ing that faces the athletic field?

What color are the curtains on this window?

Are the pillars in the first floor vestibule round or
square?

How many pillars are there?

And so forth.

Of the fifty-four answers none was entirely correct.
Students who had been at the university for one or two
years could give no better answers than those who had
recently arrived.

Of fifty-four students forty-four denied the existence
of a window they passed by daily. Only two of the
students admitted that they did not know; the rest
affimed or denied without hesitation.

Other experiments made with short films demonstrate the same variation of testimony. Claparède tried
to verify his hypotheses on the involuntary variations
in testimony by creating prefabricated incidents. He
arranged for an agitator to enter the classroom in the
middle of a lecture. He is a masked individual who
gesticulates wildly and pronounces a few unintelligible
words. Claparède has him removed from the room and
everything returns to normal. The students were unaware that the event was staged. Some days later,
Claparède interrogated them on what happened and
put a dozen precise questions to them. Almost three

quarters of the answers were erroneous. A critical study of their testimony showed that the mental habits of observers considerably influence answers given in sincerity but based on poorly remembered evidence.

One bears witness like one paints a picture; a personal note is involuntarily projected on the scene being described.

We have already noted that ten painters before the Pont du Gard will paint ten different pictures. But the same bridge will be recognizable in all of them. What is extraordinary about this is the similarity rather than diversity of the paintings.

In his report Cenac draws the following conclusions, which should make us tolerant when confronted with deformations of the truth rather than labeling them lies:

1. Entirely accurate testimony is the exception,

2. The witness offers false information with the same assurance that he gives true information,

3. Witnesses are inclined to perceive the facts and reconstruct their memory of them in terms of what seems likely to them rather than what they really saw.

Consequently, the concordance of declarations by different witnesses is not always a reliable criterion. Particularly erroneous is the testimony concerning movement, color (the color of hair and eyes are rarely reported correctly), the shape of the face, numbers, and evaluation of time spans.

On this question we may say that error is the rule and precision the exception. Women, it is said, fabricate more than men in their testimony. This is not true. Woman is as good a witness as man and often more precise in remembering the color of clothing and the like. They describe people better than men. A man will be sure of what kind of car the criminal drove, but a woman will remember better what color his hair was and what kind of clothes he wore.

The testimony of children raises serious problems. Nothing is more false than the proverb that holds that the truth comes out of the mouths of little children. We have already seen how difficult it is for a child to distinguish the true from the imaginary. He is, moreover, easily influenced and tends to confuse what he dreamed with what he saw. I have often been involved in altercations where the testimony of children was a factor. And I must say that the more I see, the more skeptical I become of such testimony. In retrospect I blame myself for having accorded too much credit to what children have told me. The child is exceptionally perverse in deceiving for the pleasure of deceiving. He is a prisoner of a fantasy life that is not sharply distinguished from the truth. When we have some experience with child psychology we learn to be especially careful before believing what they in all good faith confess, especially in sexual matters. I have observed that in two out of three cases where sex is involved the child's testimony must be doubted, even though he has no intention of doing harm. This skepticism has a twofold basis: The child will sometimes deny what has unmistakably taken place—what he either witnessed or was the victim of. Secondly, the child much more frequently invents and adds to the facts, again all in good faith.

The child is more easily influenced than the adult. He is also more impressionable and the way he is questioned dictates the answer he will give. With Cenac we think that the testimony of the children loses its value if it takes the form of answers to an interrogation. He must be made to testify without being questioned. In effect, says Cenac, "interrogation is not only likely to influence the answer by reason of the form and content of the questions posed but moreover imposes on the child a framework of reference that interferes with the structure of his spontaneous way of thinking, a structure that is not necessarily the same as that of an adult. In other words, one must try to avoid forcing the child's testimony into the mold of an inquest already organized by an adult mind. Such testimony should first of all be received in its spontaneous form, whether logical or not, and then later some kind of translation might be effected."

It is clear that prudence must guide our assessment of child testimony, especially where there is any question of the extraordinary. The extraordinary is too much like the imaginary, and unconscious factors are likely to exert a great influence.

It is not our purpose here to make a detailed study of testimony from a legal point of view. We are interested in seeing how there can be an involuntary deformation of the truth in different forms of testimony.

Emotional factors play a great role in the image that the witness retroactively constructs of the incident he is called upon to give an opinion about. We encounter here two tendencies that are often contradictory. The first is external. The witness reacts emotionally to a situation he is supposed to have observed objectively. The other is internal. The witness' temperament will influence his testimony independently of the facts.

In the first case, sentiments of antipathy or sympathy will incline him to remember and forget what he wants to forget.

In the second case, the witness satisfies a profound inner drive, such as sadism, by giving incriminating testimony. Or, inversely, he might try to make the accused appear innocent as a result of a perverse tendency to self-doubt or masochistic self-identification with the accused. No witness is a perfect witness. Instinctive drives and the need for identification always make of him a more or less direct actor in the scene observed. When we take into consideration the influence of hysterical and exhibitionistic drives, identification with the aggressor or the victim can lead to extreme consequences. If we realize that these factors are operative at all the stages of testimony, we become if not skeptical at least more critical toward it. The same factors can distort the witness' perceptive powers. A kind of psychic scotoma often falls between the observation and the testimony. To ask precise details of witnesses who are manifestly delirious is to preclude all reliable testimony. When someone in a state of hallucination says: "Everyone persecutes me," we may be sure that he will be an uncertain witness to the events he observed.

What is this psychic scotoma that interferes with our memory? In ophthalmology scotoma designates an area of the retina that no longer registers visual perceptions while the rest of the retina functions normally. In psychoanalysis, it refers to the fact that there is a gap in one's consciousness, a memory void in the center of the constellation of conscious facts that are registered in the memory. Psychoanalytic experience shows that some manifestations of the superego and phenomena of repression can especially emphasize a given fact or on the contrary push it into the shadow of complete oblivion. The perceiving brain is not like a camera that records everything that passes within its purview. Man perceives and remembers with all his being, including all his psychological conflicts. So much so that in the final analysis he may unconsciously repress some of his memories. Everything he perceives and remembers is not necessarily all that he registers. With reference to this, Cenac recalls Nietzsche's phrase: "I did that, said my memory. I did not do it, said my pride. In the end my memory gave in." Like Freud, Nietzsche knew that there are more facts in the unconscious than in the conscious memory. One of my patients described an image he had seen in a dream. It was so clear in all details that I was immediately reminded of a picture I had seen in a magazine a short while before. I showed it to my patient and he straightaway identified it as the image of his dream. Yet he affirmed that he never read the magazine in question.

Further interrogation made him recall that a few days before his dream he had sat beside someone on a bus who was leafing through this same magazine. There is no doubt that the picture was registered by his retina even though he has no memory of it.

It is prudent to be constantly alerted to the ways in which testimony can be deformed by lying, bad faith, the imagination, illusion, and errors of good faith. Still, we should not be total skeptics. There are times when the witness is sincere and his testimony authentic.

As we must be critical toward the veracity of the witness, so too must we be critical toward the objectivity of him who receives the testimony. The witness may carry the weight of his unconscious prejudices, but so too does he who receives the testimony; he is just as likely to judge as much in terms of what he is as what he has heard. He who recognizes as authentic testimony only what he judges acceptable according to his personal point of view would be in bad faith and in his own way a liar. The more testimony bears on what is out of the ordinary, the more likely we are to suspect it.

We shall omit consideration here of the kind of discordant testimony that causes passionate arguments (concerning flying saucers, for example). When testimony bears on phenomena that are outside of the normal course of events, the problem becomes extremely complicated. We have already pointed out how careful we must be in accepting testimony about the extraordinary, for more than anything else this arouses passions that compromise the truth. On the other hand, it would be too simplistic to admit only testimony that is in conformity with the normal course of things. This is the critical limit of the formula cited earlier: *Mendacium est falsiloquium communi sensu reprobatum.* We have only to recall Galileo's unhappy fate in this respect.

Let us go back over the centuries and suppose that a man testified before Louis XIV that there were horseless carriages and strange metal birds that propelled themselves through the skies. He would probably have been arrested as a disturber of the peace or perhaps sent to the mental ward of the local hospital. Any testimony concerning the extraordinary is *a priori* suspect. But more suspect still would be the judge who uncritically rejected such testimony in terms of his personal frame of reference. At times rationalism escapes itself. In such cases it would no longer be rational to remain a rationalist. We must distinguish a rationalism of prudence and expectancy from a closed rationalism that would be the negation of a world in process.

But these are extreme and fortunately exceptional cases. Before accusing the witness of lying or bad faith we should dispose ourselves favorably toward him. The judge must accept his testimony critically. We must remember, too, that the judge himself can be biased and in bad faith toward the witness.

In a fine book, Jean Guitton offers a very profound analysis of testimony with reference to the life of

Christ, especially his resurrection. The rules he lays down for this extreme case, which is the very foundation of Christian dogma, are valid for all testimony. He writes: "Yet, if there do exist some events whose supreme sense can be grasped only by rising to a higher plane of existence, you must admit that if you are to understand them clearly you cannot refuse to believe in them if they are offered to you. . . . What is required is that the answer of faith be not condemned beforehand, that a preexisting philosophy, a prior conception, or an idea in the back of my mind does not render the faith impossible to the eyes of reason. It is essential that the testimony be not implicitly refuted before giving it a fair hearing."[1]

I am reminded of a celebrated scientist who dismissed the experiments of his competitors by saying that they were all refuted "before the fact" by his personal dogmas.

The foregoing is perfectly applicable to all types of testimony, including the elementary kind offered by children. If a child feels that he won't be believed no matter what, he will invent a credible lie in order to have peace. In the same book Guitton entertains the hypothesis that the first witnesses—i.e., the apostles—were mentally deranged. Would this be grounds for rejecting their testimony? Guitton has this to say: "Grant that one could determine what is normal and define what is healthy (a difficult task even for a doctor), and that the first propagators must be classified as abnormal, nevertheless, if one is faithfully to describe the appearances, one must say that these abnormal men were also able to challenge and convince level-headed people. . . . There comes a time when the word

[1] Jean Guitton, *Jesus: The Eternal Dilemma*, trans. Donald M. Antoine, Alba House, Staten Island, 1967, p. 170.

sick no longer means what we want it to. What is normal? Would not this so-called normal man reputedly of sound mind, but slow, thick-headed, skeptical, would he not be the *true* sick man because he does not correspond to the full model of humanity?"[2]

Here again Guitton is discussing the particular case of the witness of Christ, but what he says can be generally applied. The fact that the witness is mentally disturbed is no reason to reject his testimony *a priori*. This merely introduces a new element upon which the critical spirit of the judge should bear; it is not a reason to suspect the witness of lying, bad faith, or even error and then reject his testimony. Michel Cenac has some interesting observations on this matter. While the reliability of testimony by psychopaths is in general inferior to that of normal persons, he says, it is no less true that it is frequently equal or superior. The testimony of a psychopath cannot be rejected *a priori*, no matter what the nature of his illness is. The value of a psychopath's testimony is always a question of kind and cannot be determined until the extent of his credibility can be established.

All of this goes far beyond the question of juridical testimony, and it applies to all human relationships that can be thwarted by lying. It is, furthermore, equally valid for children and adults. We all know how a child who is not endowed with exceptional intellectual gifts can nonetheless recall past events in extraordinary detail. A retarded child, who is likely to miss the general picture, can often remember material details that are completely overlooked by others. Because of the impressive power of memory in many abnormal children, their parents are often mistaken about their true intellectual potential.

2 *Ibid.*, p. 147.

CONFESSION

Just as we have made a critical study of testimony in light of lying and bad faith, so too should we undertake a similar study of confession. Confession interests me more from an educational than a legal viewpoint, although the problem usually arises in a legal context. The medico-legal aspect of confession was treated by the Congress of Alienists and Neurologists at their Geneva meeting of 1956. In his report, Dr. G. Deshaies emphasized a certain number of facts that set in relief the incidence of mendacity and veracity with respect to confession. Deshaies writes: "Phenomenologically, it is a question of a lived drama of guilt. Involved in a criminal situation, the guilty person lives an inner drama in which his conscience both accuses and absolves him. If we add the external drama of accusation, the ego can rarely resist this double constraint that confession frees it from. Confession[3] frees one from the past and commits one to the future. It reestablishes the objective unity of the criminal event and restores the continuity of the social system."

This last sentence is not only a point of criminology; it also has practical applications in family education. Parents are too often inclined to demand confession uniquely to restore the continuity of the family social system, which was disturbed by a reprehensible act. Peace, it is thought, can be restored only on condition that a confession is obtained. But such forced confessions are likely to be merely a means to achieve peace rather than effective therapy. One of my patients, a woman of thirty, was irremediably scarred because as a

[3] Experience shows that 80 percent of the guilty confess, 15 percent constantly deny, and 5 percent make inconsistent declarations. (Statistics from Deshaies.)

child she was forced to admit a theft she did not
commit. The only reason she confessed was to obtain
peace and to put an end to an intolerable climate of
family tension. We have already mentioned in speaking
of the climates of lying those family tribunals where
not only lying but also confession becomes an ineluctable necessity as a result of an accusation that grants
no quarter. Not all guilty persons are equally capable
of confession. G. Deshaies insists on the individual
psychology of different criminals. "Murderers are more
likely to confess if they acted out of emotion or passion. The personality makes a difference. Mental
debility favors false confessions and retractions. Emotional factors lead to confession as they lead to crime.
The kinds of confession admit of wide variation: emotional, logical (rational and utilitarian confessions),
expansive (vindictive, justificatory, or egotistical confessions), primitive (suicidal or redemptive confessions),
oblational (altruistic and sacrificial confessions)."

An accused person's confession is no proof of his
guilt. It is merely a presumption, which is important
but by no means categorical. Just as a witness can
falsify his testimony by lying and bad faith, so too
confession can be a countertruth—although for very
different reasons. In some cases it may be a question of deceitful (although generous) confession on the
part of someone who is wrongly accused. At the risk of
dishonor he assumes another's guilt in order to save his
life or reputation or to serve a cause that would be
compromised if the real culprit were discovered.[4]

In other cases a Kafka-like masochism may impel
one who is innocently accused to confess to what he
did not do. Again, he may do so as a result of mythomania, for there can be mythomania in confession as

---

[4] Simenon's novel *Le Fils* is the story of a father who pleads guilty
to his son's crime in order to save him.

well as in accusation. Exhibitionism can also manifest itself in confession. Dostoevski's novels abound in examples of this sort. Too, some criminals have a deep desire to be caught and do everything possible to get arrested: They may have a compulsive need to talk about themselves or play the hero. They would rather be condemned to death than remain silent or unknown.

In other cases, finally, some types confess as a result of torture (physical or emotional) in order to have peace. Some forms of interrogation differ little from torture and end by forcing the accused to confess.

Are truth serums, which act chemically on the brain, any guarantee that testimony will be free of error? No such serum exists. The mythomaniac remains a mythomaniac even under the narcosis of a so-called truth serum. This fact was observed by a number of psychiatrists at the Congress of Nice in 1955 in a report on confession. M. J. Trillot reported that criminals who have constructed a system of defense do not change it even under drugs. No psychiatrist at the present time places any faith in truth serums. As for machines such as lie detectors, it is obvious that an innocent subject can under certain circumstances give the most positive evidence of insincerity.

We cannot discuss here the problem of veracity in those who have suffered serious cerebral traumas. But there is no doubt that serious personality disorders (such as those resulting from lobectomies) can bring about profound perturbations in the value of testimony and confession. To return to an educative level, we must sketch an ethics of confession. Confession, as an expression of repressed truth, can have different values as we pointed out. Confession can reestablish a normal state of affairs; it can be necessitated by the moral conscience; there can be confessions of weakness for the purpose of obtaining peace. The latter can have disastrous consequences. E. Minkowski has studied this problem in some depth. He insists from both the psychological and educational points of view on the importance of the emotional tonality of confession. He writes: "A *sincere* lie on the part of a child has more value than flaccid, atonic, or inconsistent confessions." A sincere lie can be the basis of a constructive dialogue. Once a confession of weakness has been made it is difficult to return to the past, although criticism of lying can serve as a point of departure for a useful dialectic. Let us never admit that there is more value in a lie than in a true confession. On the other hand, if we are confronted with a lie or a refusal to confess, let us know how to make use of them. There is a good use of faults as there is a good use of sickness. In a complete treatment of this subject we would have to consider the role of confession in curing neurotic states. For isn't neurosis (from the Freudian point of view) an unconscious refusal to confess and isn't psychoanalytic therapy the means by which the patient is led to confess to himself?[5]

[5] We might point out that the confession of sins is a totally different case. Confession and psychoanalysis have nothing in common, although there is no doubt that some neurotics use the confessional to exhibit their faults—real or imagined—as a consequence of masochistic drives.

8

The Unreal: Myth,
the Imaginary, and Fiction

WE SAW in our first chapter that however paradoxical it may appear the child can accede to the truth by way of the imaginary. The imaginary can enrich the truth; it can also deform it, even suppress it altogether and replace it. Imagination is not the only faculty that can actualize truth's dynamism, but it is one of the more powerful. We make progress only when we go beyond the acquired, and the imagination is the wind that carries us to new levels of achievement. But it can also carry us astray. The wise Malebranche said that the imagination is the folly of logic. It opens the windows to let in light; but it can also permit the winds of disorder to enter. Pascal scorned the imagination. "It is that deceitful part in man, that mistress of error and falsity, the more deceptive that she is not always so; for she would be an infallible rule of truth, if she were an infallible rule of falsehood." Pascal denounces the dangers of the imagination but also notes its advantages: "This arrogant power, the enemy of reason, who likes to rule and dominate it. . . . She makes men happy and sad, healthy and sick, rich and poor; she compels reason to believe, doubt, and deny; she blunts the senses, or quickens them; she has her fools and sages. . . . What but this faculty of the imagination dispenses reputation, awards respect and veneration to persons, works, laws, and the great? How insufficient are all the riches of the earth without her consent!"[1]

We cannot conceive of a thinking world that is not at the same time an imagining world. Teilhard de Chardin's Noosphere is not only centripetal, based on a reflexive mode of thought, but also centrifugal, intuitive and creative because it projects itself outward.

The ineluctable necessity of an imaginary world results in the fact that all men find themselves necessarily confronted with two forms of unreality: One is behind them and is constituted by myths and symbols; the other is in front of them and is the product of creative imagination. The reader may be surprised to see such a subject treated in a book of this nature. But it is really very closely associated with the theme of truth and falsehood.

MYTH

It is appropriate for several reasons to begin our study of the imaginary with some considerations of myth.

Nothing can falsify a child's sense of truth as much as a mixture of what is real and true with what is not. Such a mixture, especially in the religious domain, creates doubt and in the end leads to either a religion that

[1] Blaise Pascal, *Pensées*, trans. W. F. Trotter, The Modern Library, New York, 1941, pp. 30–31.

is more magical than profound or a materialistic rationalism or skepticism.

I will not undertake a critical study of myth here. Rather I will try to warn the reader against certain false positions that can generate trouble.

What, then, is myth?

Can one live completely independent of myth?

Must we do away with myths because they do not correspond to objective truth? In which case wouldn't the myths we kill give birth to new myths?

These questions must be answered. The etymology of the word *myth* is of interest. *Muthos* in classical Greek meant a fable or legend, but to Homer and preclassical Greek it meant discourse or narrative. An even more ancient meaning was "to remember, consider, reflect." Likewise, the word *muthologein* originally meant "to narrate" but gradually came to mean *lying.*

Even in idiomatic English "to tell a story" means to lie.

Thus from the noble meaning of memory and reflection the word degenerated to a synonym of fable and lying. When classical Greek literature reworked the meaning of myth, it cut it off from its original roots and emptied it of its original dynamic meaning. Myths cannot withstand civilizations. But can civilizations survive without myths? An important current of contemporary thought is striving to reconstruct the original meaning of myths.

The foregoing explains why it is difficult to understand the value of myths. The great historian of religions Mircéa Éliade begins his book on this subject by demonstrating how the concept of myth has evolved. For a long time scholars studied myth guided by the assumption that it was fictive and unreal. In this sense it is easy to see myth as a kind of collective lie intended, if not to deceive directly, at least to reinforce through fabrication certain religious or parareligious ideas.

But today experts on this question do not consider myth fiction. As Éliade points out, they view it, on the contrary, as an expression of true history that is given special emphasis because it is sacred, exemplary, and meaningful.

Still, myth still connotes unreality to many. What I would like to stress is that myth represents the permanence of a fundamental and true idea presented in a fictional form.

It is interesting to note the evolution of philosophical thinking on myth in the past few decades. After a period of rationalism during which myth was a synonym for the irrational and error, a number of thinkers today are looking upon it as something necessary and positive. Myth is viewed as a link between man and realties that are superior and external to him. We might say as did Kierkegaard that the role of myth is to maintain the idea of eternity within the categories of time and space. This does not mean that all myths are to be retained; it simply means that behind every myth there can be a kernel of truth that cannot be reached in any other way.

Again I want to stress that from my perspective myth can and must have an educative value in the highest sense of the term and that it must not be understood solely as a lie or an error. The trick here is to distinguish the truth expressed in myth from its symbolic form. There is a kind of dialectic of myth. In order to retain its value and take on its full symbolic richness it must be demythologized, so to speak. But demythologization pushed to its limits would deprive myth of its substance, leaving nothing but a meaningless legend. But myth in the sense of symbol is an important part of modern thought. As Pradines says: "There are myths and myths. If we were to condemn all myth we would have to condemn all religion and all reason. The power of symbolism can indeed become a pitfall for thinking, but it can also be a fertile source."

Myth is a two-edged sword because it can absorb, deform, and hide the truth, but it can also be the only means of discovering it.

Many contemporary philosophers insist on the positive value of myth. Thus Gusdorf writes: "Viewed in its lived context, myth is the spontaneous form of man-in-the-world; it is neither theory nor doctrine but a concrete grasp of things, of oneself and other beings' behavior and attitudes. It is a means by which man inserts himself into reality." The restoration of myth's original dynamism is an achievement of existential thinking.

The systematic elimination of mythic thought in the name of a rational truth can lead to both religious and philosophical nonsense. H. Duméry has pointed out that the word myth as it is used technically by the phenomenologists of religion no longer means fable. It means "the *representation* of an imaginative structure with a *grasp of values*."

My intention here is to bring out the educative value of myth. Could children or adults be given an authentic religious formation without recourse to mythic expressions? The Catholic Church has long been reluctant to admit the term myth for fear of endangering historical truth.

To recognize the mythical character of some biblical passages does not mean that we must reject the profound truth of those passages. The Creation narrative in the first chapters of Genesis can be considered an expression of mythical truth. All myth, moreover, is a more or less symbolic expression of the truth of man's origins.

It pertains to specialists in exegesis to study the relationship between mythic form and historical truth. My discussion here is not intended to elucidate a problem in which I have no competence but rather to show that the total suppression of myth would lead to an impoverishment and an eventual amputation of the truth. The study of myth should be undertaken with both a critical spirit and a certain innocence. A critical sense will protect us from error; innocence, which was described by Kierkegaard as the attitude of one who does not know, disposes us to receive the truth.

Nor must we confuse mythic form with the mythological contamination found in many ancient texts that go back to common sources. Thus the ancient heroes mentioned by Genesis and the titans and giants of numerous myths stem from a tradition that is lost in the mists of prehistory. Likewise the person of Samson. While he may have been an historical figure, his exploits bear a resemblance to the myth of Hercules in Greek antiquity and, still further back in history, the Gilgamesh of the Sumerian age. Goliath was also an historical figure but has been mythologized as a physical superman less like Nietzsche's *Übermensch* than such comic strip figures as Superman and Tarzan. Saint George is not unlike those demigods who exterminate dragons and monsters. So much so that the Church no longer lists him in her hagiography.

It is altogether too easy to dismiss the historical truth of the Scriptures because it is commingled with a mythic element. Historians are those competent to discuss the authenticity of such truth. They know, too, that myth is part of a broad, realistic conception of history because it is the only history of origins we have.

The present problem is neither to reject or accept mythic expressions as such; it is rather to discuss the truth they express symbolically.

Myth as "a figuration of the divinity in his dealings with the world of men" (Malevez) is a requirement of all living religions in which communication between a personal God and his creatures is postulated. This does not exclude the necessity of a certain demythologization. The latter is sometimes necessary in order to make the historical truth of an incarnate religion clearer.[2]

But it would be erroneous to think that the imagination of men created the myths that gave rise to religions. The reverse of this is the case. It was the necessity of religious communication that created myth. This, at any rate, is Bergson's position in *The Two Sources of Morality and Religion*. The religious spirit antedates mythic creation.

We said above that a demythologized civilization would be in danger of extinction. A religion that rejects myth would be no more than a philosophy. Indeed it would not even be philosophy but a mode of thinking without reference to the transcendent. Myth has value only when interpreted in dynamic, realistic, and creative terms. As Malevez[3] says: "The historian or philosopher of religion will not deny that myth promotes a sense of mystery and can be a true expression of the divine." But, Malevez goes on to caution, the symbolic and historical forms of myth have nothing of truth about them.

In their sacred forms myths transcend the normal climate of our lives, but their spatial figuration is necessary for us to understand them. The credal phrase

[2] Henri Bergson, *The Two Sources of Morality and Religion*, trans. R. Ashley Audra and Cloudesley Brereton, New York, 1935.
[3] R. P. Malevez, *Le Message chrétien*, P.U.F., p. 1067.

descendit ad infernos . . . ascendit ad caelos is a clear expression of the mythic need to spatialize. Moreover, myths rarely have anything to say about present realities. Most often they speak of origins or what will take place at some future, unspecified time. Even in Marxist theory the golden age is to come in the future. It is something for tomorrow. Marxism urges man to work today for something that transcends his temporality.

We have discussed the question of myth at some length primarily to show that mythic thinking cannot be eliminated in the name of lying or error and that the reduction of the notion of truth to what is objective and tangible curtails it drastically by eliminating the dimension of transcendence.

There is something sacred about every myth. That is why there is always something that separates and is separated. But there is also something that binds, that builds a bridge. In this perspective, myth becomes a dialectical instrument between man and what transcends him. Mere fabulation has nothing mythic about it, because it is not symbolic and consequently has no meaning. Primitive peoples distinguished clearly between sacred myths and mere fables. Myth belongs to the rites of initiation and is only operative in certain circumstances and at certain ages. Not everyone has the right to evoke sacred myths. The initiation into myths is reserved to men. Women are excluded. On the other hand, mythic expressions that are not part of the sacred rites—stories, fables, legends, etc.—but form part of tribal folklore are accessible to all.

Myths did not die with the advent of the historical era; each age creates myths that contain an element of truth. The sacred myths of prehistory were concerned primarily with origins; those of the historical era have rather an exemplary value. They stress the mythic aspect of a real person in order to incarnate a certain force or a certain ideal. Charlemagne and Frederick Barbarossa are examples of this. Joan of Arc, Napoleon, and Louis XVII are in the same tradition even though there is no question about their historical existence. Some myths are expressed in a form that is altogether harmless while the truth they embody is very dangerous. The myth of Tristan and Isolde, which presents the ideal of a love that is stronger than death, is not untrue; similarly for the Germanic myths that fed the genius of Wagner. Myth can also be directly incarnated in an idea without the symbolic apparatus. The myth of race and blood so dear to the Nazis, of the divine right of kings, and the Marxist myth of happy tomorrows are examples. They are perhaps desacralized myths but are nonetheless sacred elements of a new faith.

To live without myths would be to become immobilized in an existence that is no longer a life, which is to say something confined to the narrow limits of space and time, a succession of identical days, without hope. This is the essence of mediocrity.

This is no facile paradox. It states that man cannot get in touch with eternal verities except through myth and that he creates only by the power of his imagination.

What we are saying has nothing to do with lying, because myth, in its imaginary form, does not suppress truth but expresses it. Myth as such cannot be a lie, although it can be exploited and become a form of lying, especially collective lying. There are no individual myths; they are by nature universal. Myth appeals directly to man's generous impulses and can be used dangerously to lead the masses into error. Myth brings men together; one is no longer alone. We participate in something and become actors rather than spectators. We are heroes, but we can also be prisoners. As men age they tend to feel the power of myth less; this is perhaps because they die many deaths before they take leave of life. Young people, on the other hand, are inspired by myths and die for them. For the old, myths die before they do. Yet even here many young people age before their time and, happily, many old people remain young in spirit! All of this has educative value and should be part of our education into the truth. To want to educate others into the truth by destroying myths would be contradictory; it would kill all desire for seeking the truth. It is obvious, of course, that myth as we are using it here must be understood in its fullest sense. Education should not aim to destroy myths but rather to inculcate a critical, constructive attitude toward them. Myth can teach us respect for mystery, which a skeptical and negative mentality would kill.

THE IMAGINARY

We included reverie among the perverse forms of pathological lying. This can be a way of lying to one-self by means of the imaginary; but in many cases the imagination can make creative use of reverie.

Dreams, considered as an unconscious expression of the imagination, are a form of the truth that belongs to the mystery of depth psychology. Freud had much to say on this subject. The Bible also illustrates in several instances how Yahweh used dreams to make his will and truth known.

We have already said something about the creative role of the imagination. We must now dwell on that subject at length. The imaginary is a necessary part of all conscious life, a fact that is of great relevance from an educational point of view. We must learn how to respect and develop a large imaginary potential if we hope to avoid a static conception of the truth. The imagination can lead us astray, but we hold it to be necessary to grasp the Truth and a capital T.

The Cartesian formula "I think, therefore I am" is perhaps less true than the more existential formula "I imagine, therefore I think, therefore I am."[4] Thinking without the imagination would not be creative thinking. Sartre's book has a number of rich insights into the relationships between consciousness and the imagination. Could we conceive of a consciousness, he asks, that never imagined, a consciousness that would be totally absorbed by its intuitions into reality? As Urs von Balthasar writes in his analysis of the phenomenology of truth: "Images give birth to the idea of an essence and an existence without containing either one. And yet *they exist*. Images seem to hover in an indeterminable manner between being and nothingness, between the subject and the object. For this reason they resemble the reality and unreality of myth. Image finds its original meaning in the distance it originally posits between itself on the one hand and essence and existence on the other. It is here that it finds its depth and mystery. The apparently rational rejection of the value of images would be an amputation of existence and a refusal of the totality of truth in its most existential sense."

Would a consciousness incapable of generating an image be capable of thought? And if it does not think it could not exist. But here we must with Sartre distinguish true imagination from memory and anticipation.

---

[4] Sartre writes: "It is as absurd to conceive of a consciousness which would not imagine as it would be to conceive of a consciousness which could not realize the cogito." J.-P. Sartre, *The Psychology of Imagination*, The Citadel Press, New York, 1948, p. 273.

When I recall the patient who was in my office yesterday and review in my memory his attitude, looks, clothing, speech, and the feel of his fatal tumor under my fingers, I do not create a new image. Rather I experience a situation that really existed. As Sartre says, it exists in the past, which is a real mode of existence among many others.

When I diagnose my patient's condition and predict how long he has to live, my imagination is not pure imagination; it is simply anticipation. This is like imagining what my tennis partner's next play is going to be. It is what Sartre calls a "real future," and my prediction is one aspect of reality. On the other hand, prescinding from what I know about my patient, I might imagine him at dinner with his wife and family. I know that I shall have to inform them of his condition. But I do not know how they will react. However, I can imagine their reaction. I can see the wife's tears, the despair of a son whose future will be compromised because he will not be able to continue his studies, and so forth. Or I might imagine the wife's effort to conceal her joy at the prospect of being freed from a man she did not really love.

Sartre writes: "We now can see what the essential requisite is in order that a consciousness may be able to imagine: It must have the possibility of positing an hypothesis of unreality."[5] To imagine is to accept the possibility of contradiction. We can envisage on the horizon of the image the necessity of nothingness, because all imagination is interrogation.

At bottom, even when the image is constructed of elements borrowed from reality it is in itself totally independent of reality and yet it can be a truth, indeed even a double truth: a truth of what is taking place

[5] *Ibid.*, p. 265.

within me at the moment I imagine and also the potential truth of a possible future.

This is not pure speculation, since it contains practical elements. The imaginary creates on the basis of existing elements but is totally independent of what exists.[6] The great importance of this point is that the power to imagine excludes the psychological determinism that would be the negation of all possible creation.[7] It is through the image that we take our distance with respect to the world, and some profound truths cannot be grasped unless we transcend reality.

Imagination enables man to see himself as a being in the world and at the same time independent of the world. It is one of the forms, if not the form, of our freedom in the world. The imaginary implies the transcendence of being. The spiritualist can scarcely refute the atheist Sartre when he writes: "If it were possible to conceive for a moment a consciousness that does not imagine it would have to be conceived as completely engulfed in the existent and without the possibility of grasping anything but the existent. . . . When the imaginary is not posited as a fact, the surpassing and the nullifying of the existent are swallowed up in the existent; the surpassing and the freedom *are there* but are not revealed; the person is crushed in the world, run through by the real, he is closest to the thing."[8] We might recall here Roquentin of *Nausea* smothered in the garden of Bouville under "tons and tons of existence." But when he leaves the garden he remarks that the garden smiled at him and that it *meant* something.

[6] Sartre says: "There is a two-fold requisite if consciousness is to imagine: It must be able to posit the world in its synthetic totality, and it must be able to posit the imagined object as being out of reach of this synthetic totality, that is, posit the world as nothingness in relation to the image." (*Ibid.*, p. 266)

[7] Determinism is undoubtedly part of all creation but is by no means the total explanation.

[8] *Ibid.*, p. 271.

Was the smile imaginary? Perhaps, but it was a source of poetry.

It is because the imagination is beyond present reality that it can be the future truth.

Were we to suppress the imagination there would no longer be any creativity nor progress of self. Controlling the child's imagination must not be confused with sterilizing it. On the contrary, we must do everything to develop it. Man does only what he imagines, and if he does not imagine he will miss life's greatest opportunities without even knowing it. Few truths impose themselves. Isn't it often the case that we must imagine them before we can receive them. To dispose ourselves consists in large measure in imagining the possibility of something that is not, for which we must make a place by nullifying what exists. Two aspects of the imagination are to be distinguished, although they become one in the end: to imagine oneself and to imagine. In imagining himself man makes himself and in imagining he makes something.

What does it mean to imagine?

It is to conceive of oneself other than one is. But isn't this a definition of the Bovary complex as given by Jules de Gaultier and as we described it in our chapter on pathological lying? It must be recalled that we denounced only abusive cases in which one pathologically imagines himself other than he is. But if we imagine ourselves other than we are in a constructive fashion, in an effort to better ourselves, there is nothing pathological about it.

From the educational point of view, a child cannot develop unless he projects himself into the future, thus imagining himself as he will be. The unreality of an imagined future is indispensable.

He who lives without imagination merely vegetates and falls prey to regressive tendencies. It is necessary for the child to concentrate on the present, but it is also indispensable that he be conscious at every moment that this present is a step toward something else that he desires. Imagination and desire are not so different from one another. This identification points to certain psychoanalytic horizons of the libido. The imagination as we have conceived it is independent of psychological determinism. One might say that desire, the libido, is the lever of the imaginary.

When I have a young patient I always ask him: "What are you going to do with your life?" His answer is necessarily relative. He may always change his mind. But what is all important is to have some idea about the future.

It is at this juncture that as a rule the indispensable phenomena of identification make themselves felt.

We are here at the level of unreality from an absolute point of view, but from an educational point of view we are at the level of truth.

The child cannot totally invent his future. He cannot, for example, create a new personality but must project his future through identification with elements of the present. The whole problem of identification is complex, and we can treat it only briefly in this chapter.

The first objects of identification are the parents, teachers, and friends. Identification can be rendered impossible by absence, such as the death of one of the parents, or may be realized only after the parental image has been degraded. The degradation may be real or imagined on the part of the child. However, there is almost always a more or less mythical image of the parental objects of identification. When a child tries to imitate his parents he always reenacts the myth of Prometheus to some extent. The notion of myth recurs in these necessary identifications. Myths are indis-

pensable to the process of identification. Why? Because
what matters is the truth of the imagined ideal more
than the truth of simple reality. Each age, each sex,
each temperament has its myths and cultivates its
heroes. Certain historical figures—Du Guesclin, Joan
of Arc, Napoleon—represent objects of possible identification. In addition to their historical reality, a mythic
dimension accrues to them. This is the exemplary
character of myth we referred to earlier, and it is necessary in order for there to be a desire for identification. The lives of the saints, provided they are edited
with taste and discrimination, are also valuable objects
of identification.

Some may object that this is no longer the realm of
the imaginary but rather pertains to history. This is not
the case, because what is historical truth becomes
imaginary as soon as something is projected on another. Paul's father is a reality, but when Paul identifies
with him he becomes unreal and imaginary.

To imagine oneself is to project oneself into the
future, and only in this way can we progress. There is
no age when we can legitimately cease to imagine. To
grow old means we no longer imagine. Man is a project
and the project is the imaginary. To renounce the
project and the imaginary is to give up.

The unreality of myths, fiction, and the imagination
is inexhaustibly rich in the sense that it impels man to
a perpetual interrogation and a perpetual transcendence
of himself. The imaginary is unreal, but it gives birth to
the greatest realities and the greatest truths. Could a
work of art be based uniquely on reality? Is it not
necessary for a wave of imagined unreality to trans-
figure what exists into another value that would have
more truth? Reality must die in order that the artist's
imagination, although nourished by it but having
transcended it, can create a truth. In this enterprise

moderation and prudence are required. Sartre's formula may be applied here: "An image can never appear excepting on the foundation of the world and in connection with the foundation." If the work that is imagined and created is cut off from "the foundation of the world," it becomes schizophrenic and delirious. The creative liberty of the imagination does not exclude moderation, and, "although as a result of producing the unreal, consciousness can appear momentarily delivered from being-in-the-world, it is just this being-in-the-world which is the necessary condition for the imagination."[9]

In more prosaic terms, we might say that from the educational point of view the liberty of the imagination should keep its feet on the ground, even when it flies high.

FICTION

All works of art are imaginary in nature. We may even say that man makes something in the true sense of the word only insofar as he imagines. We make a statue or a book, but we execute a task or a duty. It can be admitted that a ticket collector does something; but he does not engage his imagination. It is the fact of imagining, of projecting something of one's self that gives the full meaning to the word "make": i.e., to create.[10]

We shall speak here on only two minor forms of creative fiction: fairy tales and the science fiction novel. The reason for this selection is that these two

[9] *Ibid.*, p. 269.
[10] Let us bear in mind that the Greek word for "to make" is ποιειν —which gives us our word poetry. The truth of what is created and the truth of what is imagined are one and the same.

literary genres are farthest removed from reality. We intend to show that there is creative value in even the most fanciful exercise of the imagination. Mircéa Éliade concludes his book on myth with an unexpected chapter on fairy tales. He shows that this extreme instance of fabulation is not without meaning and can be a means of directly or symbolically expressing eternal myths. Some fairy tales repeat in a desacralized and frankly fictional form the ancestral rites of initiation. The theme of death to oneself as a condition of rebirth is an example. Another is a frequent emphasis on the necessity to escape into the miraculous and break with the normal conditions of life in order to reach the happy ending that characterizes all fairy tales. Fortunately, there has been a reaction against the abusive use of fairy tales in children's literature. But we must also stress their good uses. Properly presented and emphasizing the pure play of imagination, they undoubtedly have great value in awakening the mind. Some of them, of course, can be fully appreciated only by adults. But few fairy tales fail to contain some grain of truth.

We might note here that those fairy tales that give expression to archetypical myths remind us of Jung's theory of the collective unconscious.

As Mircéa Éliade emphasizes, fairy tales are less a "desacralization" than a "degradation of the sacred." This is not meant in a pejorative sense, but rather indicates a minor register of imaginative expression. All things considered, fairy tales are no doubt preferable to fabulation. Religious legends are far more dangerous because there is no real way of telling where error ends and the truth begins. There is a whole hagiography of legends that have nothing to do with history and that have done much harm because they ignore the symbolic sense of the sacred in favor of mere pious fabulation.

Today there is another form of fairy tale called science fiction. In the tradition of the genre we find Rabelais, Jules Verne, Swift, and H. G. Wells. Science fiction has greater anticipatory content than fairy tales, a point that has been made by serious scholars. In this case, can they still be imaginary in the high sense Sartre describes? The fantasy element of such works makes them appear imaginary when in fact they do no more than extrapolate the future. Science fiction appeals to all tastes and all ages. It is written by authors of all descriptions, ranging from the anonymous to authentic researchers who present their material on a solid scientific basis. Escape is a central theme of science fiction, not only escape from the earth but also from time itself. Here there is no magic ring of the fairy tale to take us out of time, for science fiction admits of neither mystery nor the miraculous. The perspective is rigorously scientific or at least is presented as such. Theories of relativity and the fourth dimension are often appealed to. The fantastic becomes rational; everything seemingly can be explained by proven theories or established experiments. On occasion the philosophers of time are quoted, and time itself eventually becomes a function of space. The immensity of distance is an overwhelming theme of all science fiction.

Science fiction novels are often peopled with robots: an extraordinary conception of an artificial man who is entirely mechanized and seems to be possessed of intelligence (that is a sense of finality), a being capable of resolving electronically and instantaneously problems that are beyond the power of a human brain. When we realize the amazing achievements of computers, robot-man no longer seems so unthinkable. He is perhaps the beginning of a new myth: that of the domination and obliteration of man by the machine that he created in his image and that one day perhaps will shout from the rooftops: "God is dead."

Our intention here is not to write a history of science fiction but rather to try to point out its positive content, although there can be no question of truth in the absolute sense of the word. Still, science fiction represents a potential that has its truth, and we would be wrong to dismiss it because it describes unreal things. At the end of all these novels are posed more or less clearly questions that transcend scientific anticipation and deal with the problem of man, his destiny and limitations. The suggested answer might be a form of materialistic Utopianism; or it might be another question. Having reached the confines of the farthest galaxy, the hero discovers yet more distant worlds that must be explored. The greatest scientific accomplishments offer no definitive solution to the problem of man. This is a problem that no robot-man can ever raise. He may be able to solve problems, but he can never ask a question.

The truth of science fiction is not in what it describes but in the questions it forces us to ask. It is perhaps a paradox that truth should take the form of an interrogation (and therefore negation). Yet this is the truth of man: the power to question himself. Jean Pecqueur has pointed out that science fiction is healthier than police novels, which so often stir dirty waters; science fiction is also more meaningful because it affects our emotions and imagination and therefore our lives. It helps man maintain hope before the immensity of the world and encourages his technical efforts, and this is all to the good. Science fiction also warns us against the dangers of the machine—for both the individual and society—and stimulates a hope in real progress; this too is all to the good. Finally, the science fiction novel is closer to the truth than it is to lying because it can be a path to the former.

9

Lying and Professional Secrecy

AT FIRST SIGHT there is no evident relation between lying and professional secrecy. In practice, however, the one can bring about, or appear to bring about, the necessity of the other.

All professions require some measure of secrecy, particularly medicine, law, and the ministry.

As a doctor, I shall refer primarily to cases of conscience that can arise in the exercise of the medical profession.

THE DOCTOR, MEDICAL SECRECY, AND THE RIGHT OF THE PATIENT TO THE TRUTH[1]

Our subject here is not strictly speaking medical secrecy. To remain within the framework of this book,

[1] In this chapter we rely heavily on two issues of the *Cahiers Laennec*—the 1950 issue is devoted to medical secrecy while the 1957 issue deals with the right of patients to the truth—and a recent general review by Professor Grmek of Zagreb.

we shall deal solely with the problem of truth and falsehood in reference to medical secrecy.

Medical secrecy is strictly binding and is prescribed by law. It is the honor of the medical profession.[2] It is, moreover, an essentially negative obligation: It obliges one not to speak. It is almost always easier not to speak than to speak. However, there are silences that are more eloquent than confessions. To barricade one-self behind silence is sometimes implicitly to admit that "there is something." Theoretically, there is no secrecy between a doctor and his patient. The problem arises with respect to those who "have the right" to the doc-tor's confidence. There is, it would seem, no problem as far as parents, children, and spouses are concerned. But how should this be interpreted? It is difficult to set precise guidelines for those who would exploit the truth, even though they have a right to it.

It is not our purpose to enter into a legal discussion on the limits and denotation of "those who have the right." We are condemned to silence, a silence that no one can take away from us, not even the patient who sometimes cannot foresee the extent of the conse-quences were the prohibition lifted. The doctor's si-lence, as we have said, can become a confession, unless there is some intention to deceive. But it seems worth noting that some degree of lying can be attributed to a silence that deceives the interlocutor.

Here are two examples. Mr. X's daughter is going to marry Mr. Y's son. Mr. X came to see me and said: "I know that you have treated my future son-in-law. His family assures me that it is nothing serious. What is your opinion?" It is true that there was nothing seri-

---

[2] We could give many examples from the recent past of doctors who chose to resign from the profession rather than compromise their pro-fessional responsibility under pressure from ignorant or irresponsible administrators.

ously wrong with the young man; but I *absolutely do not have the right* to tell Mr. X anything about his case. Yet my silence might deceive Mr. X. He could draw the conclusion that since I won't talk about it, it must have been serious. In another case a certain man came to see me with an identical story. But in this case I had treated the future son-in-law for a very serious schizophrenic condition, which appears to have been only temporarily arrested. Again, I *absolutely must remain silent*. My silence could deceive this gentleman into thinking that if it were really a question of something serious I would tell him. Since I did not, he will be reassured.

I have seen many impossible marriages contracted because I could not violate my oath of professional secrecy. Some might think that my duty was to dissuade seriously ill patients from marriage. Otherwise don't I refuse him a part of the total truth and therefore lie? On the other hand, might not the total truth have even more serious consequences? It might, for example, lead to suicide. Can I be sure of the finality of a truth that is only a probability in view of a patient's present condition and in the present state of a science that is ever progressing? Thus counseling someone not to marry under any circumstances could be a countertruth.

This brings us to the central problem of the patient's right to the truth and the interferences with this right by what has been called the doctor's white lies. This discussion is relevant to our study of truth and falsehood. The day comes for all of us when we will want to know the truth from our doctor. And every doctor is sooner or later torn between his duty to tell the truth and his desire to be charitable.

Before taking up the question of the doctor's right to tell a white lie, let us try to see if a charitable lie is really a lie and inquire into its legal status. According to the strict definition of lying there can be no subterfuges. Thus the doctor's white lie would in all cases be reprehensible. Kant was one philosopher who took this strict position. According to Grotius, who defines lying to be withholding a *truth that is due*, the case is a little different. But here again we must be clear: Is it merely a question of not telling the truth to those who have no right to it or of arrogating to oneself the right to "arrange the truth," to disguise and dissimulate it?

We saw earlier that considerable attention must be paid to the character of the person lied to. This is maximally important with respect to the sick—whether it be a question of a travesty of the truth or mere silence, which is in itself deceptive.

We need not adopt the cynical attitude of Voltaire—who said that lying is wrong only when it does harm and is a great virtue when it does good. On the other hand, we must not fall into a rigorous legalism that would perhaps put the doctor outside the laws although not outside of his conscience, for there are some truths that kill. R. Savatier, a professor of law, has on several occasions in his writings attacked the pretension of doctors who decide what must be told and done to patients on the basis of norms that are not contained in the legal code. He expresses indignation toward the "medical imperialism" that not only violates the law but also the rights of persons. This is a splendid example of the gap that separates the professor who pronounces dogmas, enacts laws, and formulates sanctions in theory from the doctor by a patient's deathbed who is bound to remain within the limits of the useful, the possible, and the human. But Professor Savatier does admit of attenuating circumstances. He admits that there is "a great difference between the prohibition of countertruths and the obligation to tell a patient the whole truth." The patient has a right to more than "useful truth." On the other hand, "one does not disguise the truth in adapting it to the person who receives it." This is a very broad interpretation of *veritas debita*. Let us add to this that the doctor can never affirm the absolute character of either his diagnosis or his prognosis. He knows that science progresses rapidly and what he affirms today may well be denied tomorrow. This imposes great modesty upon him as well as great flexibility in applying principles. Confronted with the same case, the most rigorous lawyer and the doctor could likely agree on what course of action to follow, especially in light of the changing character of medical knowledge. Any doctor today who did not warn pregnant women of the extreme dangers of German measles would be lying, although a few years ago no one would have reproached him. Similarly, for other diseases. Today some things are obligatory for doctors that were not forty years ago.

Here we are no longer in the domain of lying, yet an awareness of possible error often imposes attitudes and words that are more the truth of yesterday than of today. Less than thirty years ago a doctor who gave any hope for a child stricken with tubercular meningitis would have been judged an impostor, a charlatan or, at the very least, ignorant. Now all that has changed. Today it would be criminal not to have hope for a cure. Who knows, perhaps at the very moment I judge a disease terminal there is a cure for it in some laboratory. If I give more grounds for hope than I myself believe justified, am I a liar? Would my moral conscience be more comforted if I rely on present knowledge without looking to the future? What must be done in each particular case is to consider all sides of the problem and then decide upon what attitude to take, and this less in terms of principles than of a sensitive moral conscience, which in the final analysis can be judged only by itself (even if from the legal point of view it is not totally free from the judgment of men and the sanction of the laws). Is a strictly legal practice of medicine possible or even desirable? Nothing paralyzes a nation more than the zeal of those charged with applying the laws. The doctor's first responsibility is to treat the patient, and some lying may be necessary to enable him to do this. He must in the final analysis measure truth and falsehood by what is good for the patient, provided the latter's material and spiritual interests as well as those of his family are respected. We must never forget that the patient before us also has his truth, and beyond him and us there is a still greater truth. This is much more important than worrying about legal subtleties.

In a well-documented article on the white lies of doctors, Professor Grmek cites the Church Fathers. St. Hilary says a lie can be justified to comfort a patient. St. John Chrysostom puts lying on the same level as the knife, the iron, and poison—all of which can be used for the good of the patient. Pius XII admits that a doctor, although he is not permitted to say what is positively false, can withhold the truth, especially when he knows that the patient will not have the strength to accept it. Let us consider further this particularly authoritative advice. What are we to understand by a patient who is not strong enough to accept the truth? This question can be viewed from two different positions. First, is the patient mature enough to accept the truth without dissimulation? Secondly, admitting that he could do so in a normal state of health, does the fact that he is ill make a difference?

The first question brings out a fundamental problem: Are many patients sufficiently mature to accept the truth of their fulfillment in death? I doubt it. Both believers and unbelievers have great difficulty in doing so and prefer the lie that puts death off rather than the truth that brings it near. The following anecdote is to the point. An aged priest's housekeeper said to him one day:

"Father, I dreamed that you were in heaven."

"How fortunate," said the priest.

"I also dreamed that you would die tomorrow," the housekeeper added.

"How unfortunate," sighed the venerable priest. A white lie would undoubtedly have been more acceptable to him. The lies that doctors are forced to tell are determined more by the patient's condition than the doctor's bad will. Most patients haven't thought enough about death to be able to accept it when it comes. Because men lie to themselves—whether voluntarily or involuntarily—all through life, they cannot accept the truth when their time has come. One does not have to lie to those who have reflectively integrated death into their lives. Not everyone is prepared for the truth, and law books omit mention of this fact.

Dr. Malgras has some excellent observations on this subject. "Too often," he says, "we do not trust our patients enough, we do not believe in the possibilities that lie dormant in them. Because we do not want to discourage them, we remain silent. But if we knew how to tell them the truth and at the same time comfort them, then we would have to change our views. We must of course be prudent. Patients who best accept the truth about their condition are often those who seem most afraid. On the other hand, those who seem most courageous sometimes become totally confused when confronted with the fact of their own death. Let us beware of the man who says: 'Doctor, I am strong. You can tell me everything.' Behind the affirmations, we must learn how to discover the character of each patient. It is not true that a believer who has frequented the sacraments regularly will always accept the advent of death serenely. A very religious woman was seized with panic when I informed her that she would have to undergo a dangerous operation. I retain the painful memory of a remarkable social worker with a deep religious fervor who refused for months to admit that a cancer of the breast had become generalized. That is why during this period of anguish, awareness of danger and sometimes outright rebellion, the patient needs to be comforted, not with lies or artificial politeness but with an authentic understanding that will enable them to accept their condition and recover their calm."

That second limiting factor in considering the truth due to a sick person is the extent to which his condition has diminished his ability to accept the total truth. This is a very delicate question, for most of the time patients think they are strong enough while the doctor may judge differently. It may be objected that the doctor takes too much upon himself in judging the limits of his patient's psychological resistance, especially when personal considerations are involved. It is true that a patient cannot be treated like an alien or a minor in all cases. Yet it is very possible that, temporarily or definitively, his condition may impel him to prefer a lie to the truth for his own good. Legalists are not very sensitive to this kind of argument and have difficulty admitting that there can be, from the point of view of the patient's interest, legitimate reasons to avoid telling the total truth. As long as the medical profession is in its present state of progress it is always possible that we doctors will be proven wrong.

There is a politics of frankness with patients that is sometimes no more than a politics of the open umbrella. We protect ourselves with the good conscience of total sincerity so that later on when the winds are contrary we can say: "I told you everything." This is the cunningness recommended by the school of Salerno, which advised the doctor to say: "Promise the patient that you will cure him with God's help but inform his family of the seriousness of his condition. In this way, if he is cured, you will be praised. If he dies, you will have witnesses that you held out little hope."

A doctor cannot always be a legalist. He must always be concerned with the truth but knows from experience that the truth of the moment may not be the eventual truth he envisages in the interests of his patient.

Having made the foregoing distinctions ought I not now make my own position clear? I believe that it is in all cases the *integrity* of the truth that should govern a doctor's attitude toward his patients. But this is possible only on two conditions. The first is this: Admit that any lie is merely a means of achieving an eventual truth. Secondly, do everything possible to dispose the patient to accept the total truth about himself in the end. This is an essentially dynamic conception of the truth. Let us never promise more than we can back up and let us never forget that science has not yet had the last word. And beyond science there is a mystery of life that transcends both the patient and his doctor. If what seems like a lie today respects the truth of this mystery, is it still a lie? But even in this perspective, a lie must be the exception—not an end that hides the truth but a means to attain it. Let us recall Plato's words in *The Republic:* "Truth should be highly valued. If, as we were saying, a lie is useless to the gods, and useful only as medicine to men, then the use of such medicines should be restricted to physicians. Private individuals should have no business with them." If the wise Plato accords the disciples of Hippocrates a kind of monopoly on the right to dissimulate, let us not abuse it and resort to it only infrequently.

The experience of daily practice and common sense will generally indicate the best solutions. The doctor's competence, his humility and charity, his respect for the transcendence of the person of his patient, and a concern for his material and spiritual interests will of themselves dictate the course of action to be followed. If there is a conflict between the law and a doctor's conscience, the latter must in the final analysis prevail. Only in this way can he be loyal to his patient and faithful to his art. As Pascal put it: "The abuse of truth ought to be as much punished as the introduction of falsehood. As if there were two hells, one for sins against love, the other for those against justice."[3]

THE LAWYER, LYING, AND TRUTH

The general public seems to be of the opinion that a lawyer has the right to take liberties with the truth and that all arguments, including the most fallacious, can be used to defend the client and defeat the prosecution. But this is not the case. It is not our intention here to discuss the principles of a profession whose origins go back to the dawn of history. While the Hippocratic oath remains the basis of medicine, the principles that regulate the legal profession have been revised many times. The capitularies of Charlemagne stipulated that lawyers should be meek, peace-loving, God-fearing, and lovers of justice. In addition to professional secrecy the lawyer may be caught between his duty to be an auxiliary of justice and the obligation to defend

[3] Pascal, *op. cit.*, p. 318.

his client. The revised code of St. Louis urged the lawyer to present no dishonest case—a first reference to truth. The lawyer must be honest in the causes he defends as well as in his behavior.

A specialist in legal principles has written in a chapter on general duties: "Truth is another obligation that flows from probity. It obliges the lawyer to cite only true evidence and prohibits him from having recourse to dissimulations. While one may not be obliged to tell everything, one never has the right to dissimulate. There is sometimes only a slight difference between honest reticence and dissimulation, but it is a major one from the point of view of conscience."[4]

The classic work of Payen insists on the same principle: The lawyer can never speak against the truth. He can point out the different aspects of truth and stress those that are in the best interests of his client. If the client insists that he lie, the lawyer can—and perhaps must—refuse to oblige. But once he has accepted a client he must follow his instructions. This is a situation that can create serious moral problems for a lawyer.

Payen also notes the special position of a lawyer vis-à-vis an accused who confesses. The accused may have confessed untruthfully for reasons we explained in our chapter on testimony and confession [Chap. 7]. Here is what Payen says: "Despite such confessions and contrary to the authority of many legal experts, the lawyer can plead for acquittal in such cases. He can do this not only in law but also in conscience. The question addressed to the jury is not whether a crime has been committed but whether the accused is guilty, whether he had criminal intent and should be punished." This principle gives the lawyer the liberty to

4 M. Mallot, *Abrégé des règles de la profession d'avocat*, 1867.

doubt the veracity of confession if there are good reasons for doing so.

Professor Louis Crémieu speaks in a similar vein when he stresses the lawyer's loyalty. He is professionally bound to assure the good functioning of the public service of justice in which he participates. This loyalty demands veracity. As Crémieu puts it: "Loyalty implies veracity. In the exercise of his profession, the lawyer must scrupulously avoid tampering with the truth. . . . The affirmation of false facts and inexact quotations of legal texts or other sources constitute serious offenses. . . . In penal matters the lawyer must sort out the true from the false. He must try to discover the truth in order to be able to plead with conviction; but he must abstain from all pressure when his client has admitted his guilt to him. He must never divulge this under pain of violating his professional oath. But if such a client should ask him to plead his innocence, then the lawyer is bound in conscience either to resign the case or to limit himself to pointing out the doubtful aspect of the prosecution's case."

These different opinions show that there can be no justification for lying in the legal profession. Professor Crémieu often told his classes: The lawyer may be partial, but he must never be untruthful. Pascal said that "the feeble-minded are people who know the truth, but only affirm it so far as consistent with their own interest."[5] Not all lawyers would fall into this category.

The profession of law sorely tries the virtue of loyalty, but from what I have been able to observe lawyers are as a whole conscientious men and are on the whole successful in overcoming conflicts of interest when they arise.

[5] Pascal, *op. cit.*, p. 191.

LYING AND THE CONFESSIONAL SEAL

It does not lie within our competence to discuss the sacrament of confession as such. We have seen that the doctor and lawyer can be tempted to dissimulate the truth in the exercise of their profession. Is this true of the confessor? Does he have the right to withhold the truth either partially or totally?

Here is one expert's opinion. After stressing the fact that difficulties in this respect are extremely rare, he says: "In order to strictly observe the secrecy of the confessional when one is 'cornered,' it may be necessary to avoid adroitly certain questions or even to answer in terms that do not conform with what one knows to be the objective truth. One must not hesitate in this, or even appear to hesitate for it is a case of 'legitimate defense.' The legitimate defense of this secret can justify an adaptation, bending, or even dissimulation of the truth. One must apply an analogous and equally strict rule with regard to the use made of knowledge acquired in the confessional, which if divulged, even for the best of reasons, would endanger the sacramental seal."

The same professor stresses the importance for a priest to avoid putting himself in compromising situations. Thus, insofar as possible, he will avoid offering spiritual guidance to both husband and wife. Spiritual direction is normally given in the confessional or in any case is an extension of it.[6] A pastor in a small parish may have to hear the confessions of both husband and

---

[6] More and more the confession and spiritual direction are becoming two separate functions. A spiritual director and a confessor need not be the same person.

wife. In that case he should be extremely prudent when talking to them in a guidance situation.

We might note that, for similar reasons, a psychiatrist would be well advised not to treat both husband and wife.

10

The Prevention of Lying and Bad Faith:

Love of Truth

> *Truth is so obscure in these times, and false-*
> *hood so established, that unless we love the*
> *truth, we cannot know it.*—PASCAL

IF CERTAIN NEUROSES can be cured by a therapy that reveals their unconscious motivation, can it also be said that nonpathological lying can be prevented by inculcating certain attitudes and behavior patterns?

From what we have said previously two broad principles can be deduced from the fact that there are climates of lying and the fact that the intentionality of lying supposes some interest. If we suppress the climates that make lying inevitable and see to it that lying can serve no utilitarian purpose, we will have contributed greatly to its prevention. Furthermore, we would have to suppress the desire of lying for lying's sake, that appetite for gratuitous evil, evil for itself. Pascal emphasizes this when he writes: "Although people may not have anything to gain from what they are saying, we must not absolutely conclude from this that they are not lying; for there are some people who lie for the mere sake of lying."[1]

---

[1] Pascal, *op. cit.*, p. 43.

We must distinguish the climates of lying from its utilitarian uses. A climate of lying leads to the falsification and dissimulation of the truth. In such a climate life cannot be lived without deception. This is the atmosphere that makes the utilitarian lie necessary. Viewed in this perspective, lying seems reasonable and becomes a means of adaptation and survival.

What we must strive to do, therefore, is to deprive lying of its usefulness, to make it appear so aberrant that it will no longer serve any rational purpose. A family situation in which a child could feel in harmony only by telling the truth would eliminate the necessity for lying.

But this is the essentially negative perspective of rewarded virtue. It would not be enough to eliminate lying because it is less utilitarian than the truth. This would be inferior even to a morality of prohibitions. The latter may be an expression of a superior moral stance and contain positive elements. If it were simply a question of utility, lying might be eliminated temporarily, but there is no guarantee that it might not one day become useful again. We must not conclude from this, however, that our efforts to modify the climates of lying are therefore unnecessary or that the only thing that matters is to be convinced of the evil of lying in order to resist it. Kantian voluntarism might be satisfied with such an attitude but replacing the utilitarianism of lying with a desire for virtue will effect no substantial change.

Only what is of positive value can serve as a basis for a constructive morality. A morality of prohibition, taboos, servile obedience and domination that is suffered but not accepted and still less understood is an archaic, magical morality. Openness, loyalty, sincerity, and fidelity that depend upon a constant effort of the will would soon lead to moral suffocation.

True morality draws its dynamism not from prohibition but from the strength of constructive propositions. It orients more than it condemns. Thus understood, morality is not a barrier but an appeal, an opening.

The educator must *make the truth loved* and he can do so only to the extent that he loves it himself and lives it with his whole being.

THE LOVE OF TRUTH

The most effective way to prevent lying is to set the truth in glaring relief. The passion for truth—a passion that is intelligent, always charitable and never intransigent—cuts the roots of lying. It is not a question of making truth an idol. "We make an ideal of truth itself; for truth apart from charity is not God, but His image and idol, which we must neither love nor worship; and still less must we love or worship its opposite, namely, falsehood."[2] The love of and passion for truth must be tempered by charity, which remains the measure of all things. If we should indulge our passion for truth but lack love for those to whom we wish to make it known, we would not be truthful.

Passion for the truth must be further tempered by the realization that each age has its own truth. The child understands prohibitions before he comes to love the truth. Each age has its partial truth that does not deny the totality of the truth but must be presented differently at different stages of development. Truth must be given the form that corresponds to each step of evolution. We must never compromise with error for reasons of expediency or the desire to explain everything. I cannot accept one of Pascal's sayings in which he seems to grant the value of a common error

[2] *Ibid.,* p. 191.

that substitutes for a true explanation and quells curiosity, although from a psychological point of view, it is true, many persons are satisfied with any answer to their question regardless of its authenticity. Here is what Pascal says: "When we do not know the truth of a thing, it is of advantage that there should exist a common error that determines the mind of man, as, for example, the moon, to which is attributed the change of seasons, the progress of diseases, etc. For the chief malady of man is restless curiosity about things that he cannot understand; and it is not so bad for him to be in error as to be curious to no purpose."[3]

Although we cannot in all circumstances arrogate the right to give a false explanation for something unexplained, it is nonetheless evident that in some cases we may be called upon to quiet another's uneasiness with an erroneous explanation.

This does not legitimize the kind of story that explains the mystery of birth by saying storks bring babies. On the other hand, there is a way in which such "lies" can have a positive use. One night during the war my daughter, then three years old, was awakened by exploding bombs. To reassure her I explained that the Baby Jesus was bowling with her recently deceased grandmother. I do not think I deceived her with this explanation. Quite the contrary. Nonetheless it remains true that an explanation based on truth is always to be preferred if possible, especially where prohibitions are involved. A prohibition that is based upon truth will be much more effective. Let us take a banal example. A mother prohibits her eighteen-month-old baby from playing with safety pins. How can the child understand this prohibition? It doesn't help if the

[3] Cf. Thought 226: "We must then talk like others but not think like them." (Also Thoughts 298 and 299.) Whatever interpretation be given to such texts, they remain puzzling.

mother explains that the pins will hurt the child. But if she applies the pinpoint lightly to the child's finger, he will understand immediately the reason for the prohibition. This contact with reality will make the child understand that the truth of the pin is to prick. This is admittedly a simple example, but it can be a first introduction to a concern for the truth. Here we see that the love of the truth goes hand in hand with the love of learning, knowing, and understanding. Must we conclude from this that the passion for truth cannot be disassociated from the passion for understanding and that to inculcate a taste for the truth in children is at the same time to explain everything to them? This is one of the most difficult questions related to the passion for truth. But we must bear in mind that it is also a truth to teach the child that he is not able to grasp everything at once. An important part of education is to teach the child the essential truth that he is a person in a state of becoming and that there will always be a tomorrow when truths that are unclear today will be understood more clearly. This notion of truth in a state of constant becoming, which is not to be confused with constant mutation, is indispensable for a healthy love of the truth: a truth that is not only perceived and assimilated today but is at the same time a truth that will be perceived and understood more deeply tomorrow. This leads to a dynamic conception of truth and precludes the possibility of ever possessing it totally. The love of truth is more the desire for seeking it than possessing it, not in the manner of a Don Juan for whom the quest is more satisfying than the conquest but more like a pilgrim for whom the accomplished effort is of primary importance.

This objection is frequently raised: How does all of this relate to daily life with its struggles and immediate responsibilities? Let us make it clear here that there are no little truths or lies. We never know where the great conquests and the great betrayals will begin. In that admirable film *Brief Encounter* betrayal began with a grain of dust in the eye.

If we succeed in convincing others that the only sure values are truth or, better still, the search for the truth, we will have accomplished the essential. What other passions are worthwhile? What matters most in the struggle that marks every human life is the passionate pursuit of truth. We will be judged not on whether we possess or do not possess the truth but on whether or not we sought and loved it.

The possession of the truth is a terminus, an omega point in which everything becomes clear. But no one reaches it here below. This is not a skeptical but a realistic attitude. To go toward the true is already to be in the truth; we cannot go toward the important truths without passion; and this passion is rooted in the events of daily life. Passion for the truth! This was the title of a fine book by Étienne Borne.[4] Another excellent treatment is a book by Urs von Balthasar on the phenomenology of truth.[5] What follows is deeply indebted to these two authors.

THE UNITY OF TRUTH AND THE
PLURALITY OF WAYS

The passionate approach to the truth must be accompanied with the greatest humility. The truth is one, but the roads to it are multiple. It would be necessary to cite all the philosophers and thinkers of history to give some idea of mankind's efforts to acquire truth. There are those who think that this pluralistic ap-

[4] Étienne Borne, *Passion de la vérité*, Fayard, 1962.
[5] Urs von Balthasar, *Phénoménologie de la vérité*, 1952.

proach to the truth is dangerous because it introduces germs of relativism, skepticism, and absurdity. Yet each approach to the truth has its worth and contributes its stone to the total edifice.

The mystical truth of Plato and John of the Cross.

The realism of Aristotle and Aquinas.

The anxious truth of Pascal.

The logical and geometrical truth of Descartes.

The critical truth of Kant.

The dialectical and historical truth of Hegel.

The prophetic truth of Nietzsche.

The intuitive truth of Bergson.

The existential truth of Kierkegaard, Sartre, and Camus.

These various approaches are only apparently contradictory for the ways of truth are multiple. Étienne Borne stresses this in his book. It is not so much the philosophers who are contradictory; rather they express the contradictions of the human condition. Philosophy progresses through pluralism and disagreement to an eventual harmony. Nothing should be rejected *a priori*. Pascal warns us: "Contradiction is not a sign of falsity; nor the want of contradiction a sign of truth."[6]

Each system offers something; there is a constant dialectic in pluralism. While we may have a vision of the final unity we are nonetheless always in danger of losing our way and being distracted by the kaleidoscope of fragmented truths.

For this reason we need objective guidelines to mark the way to final truth. In his great conversion on the night of November 23, 1654, Pascal invoked the God of revelation and history—the God of Abraham, Isaac, and Jacob—and not the god of philosophers.

6 Pascal, *op. cit.*, p. 124.

Picking our way through the various theories of truth is undoubtedly the most difficult thing we can do. The ways are so different and choice is always agonizing. There are, to be sure, false ways, and it is by no means easy to recognize them. But there is also a false manner of taking the right roads. Perhaps the worst is the pride-inspired conviction that our way is the best way. This is of capital importance from an educational point of view, for to teach others how to discover the truth does not mean that their methods must be rejected, even though they seem to be in contradiction with our own. To respect the other's way is a form of charity. If we are convinced that he is in error, charity must still prevail when we try to convince him to revise his theories. If we sincerely try to understand the other's point of view and the way he reached it, we may discover that we erred in assuming the truth of our own perspective. Pascal puts it this way: "When we wish to correct with advantage, and to show another that he errs, we must notice from what side he views the matter, for on that side it is usually true, and admit that truth to him, but reveal to him the side on which it is false."[7] To respect the thought of each student while trying to lead all to the same end is an extremely difficult task for the teacher. It is only too human to adopt one truth and make no effort to examine the worth of others. Truth is expressed in the movement of living beings and like them is alive. But, unlike them, it never dies. We must not be intimidated by the evident risks involved in seeking the truth. All great adventures are dangerous. Truth has its brilliance; but it also has its mystery. Whoever is not disposed to receive the mystery will not likely attain the truth. Philosophers often speak of the truth that springs from the dialectic

[7] *Ibid.*, p. 7.

of this brilliance and this mystery. Is it really a dialectic? Is it not rather a complementarity? Pascal says so (cf. Thought 282). So does Borne: "Because man thinks, his mind has movement and being in the truth. But he thinks in several different ways. Thus multiplicity, contrariety, and opposition lead to the truth. Thus truth is not distant, fleeing, inaccessible; it is always under our eyes, near at hand, at the end of this tool or this equation. Or it may be just behind us. But we must never turn back for we will see nothing. Rather we must listen to its silence and understand it symbolically."

EXTERIORITY AND INTERIORITY

The reader may be surprised that we insist at such length on the various ways of attaining truth. But the whole pedagogy of truth is here. It is not so much a question of establishing certainty as of determining the means to certainty. Man never achieves final certainty. Consequently an education that did not equip him with the techniques of pursuing truth would be a failure. To give a child the principles of truth is necessary; to convince him that he must continually seek the truth is even more so.

We described in our first chapter how the child comes to the notion of the truth. We spoke for the most part of external truth and touched only briefly upon an interior sense of the truth, which for the child is almost always identified with the notion of evidence. The notion of evidence, however, does not come from a purely interior reflection; it admits of certain external elements. Freudian psychoanalysts speak here of an awareness of the reality principle.

Truth is both something that is within us and external to us. What would a purely external truth be? It can be recognized only when we participate in it and therefore appropriate it inwardly. A truth that is not known and never will be known, now or later, here or in the hereafter, is no truth at all. The light under the bushel loses its truth, for the truth of light is not to be but to shine. Children must be taught that they are participants in the truth by virtue of the knowledge they have or will have. This attitude will make lying less attractive. To deny a truth we are ignorant of is a neutral act; but to deny a truth we possess or could possess is to deny and destroy oneself.

Inversely, a truth that is purely interior, does not shine forth, and lacks support in the external world is a schizophrenic truth. It would be a truth of madness, not of reason.

A third hypothesis may be entertained: that of a truth perceived as external to the self but to which my mind makes no contribution. In this case the mind would be alienated from the truth because the person must retain his freedom before the truth.

We see here what the basis for an education to the truth must be: the transcendence of a truth that exists independently of the self but that corresponds to nothing if the self does not recognize it and appropriate it in an act of freedom.

Education into the truth must take place gradually, in a number of harmonized stages. First of all, communication to another of a truth that he cannot yet grasp; then, little by little, the development of a critical sense in him; finally, a conviction of his freedom vis-à-vis the proposed truth. The child must be made aware of concrete truth before being introduced to abstractions. He is much more apt to understand facts than speculation. That is why myth, in the broad sense we described earlier, is an excellent means of teaching the truth. It is an initial means of grounding the truth in the objective reality of historical understanding.

History is the foundation of all exteriority. But let us return now to a discussion of interiority, which is also indispensable. Even history has no truth value unless it is appropriated by the mind. The evolution of adult consciousness increasingly accommodates an awareness of interior truth. It is not so much that an interior truth is substituted for an external one. The former is more like an addition. Without playing on words we might say that interiority is an awareness of being aware of the truth. It is the transition to the "I" we discussed in our remarks on the discovery of truth.

Awareness of one's awareness and by that token an awareness of being. This is part of what Descartes' doctrine of the *Cogito* teaches. This awareness of being, the fact of knowing oneself as a thinking being, is the foundation of all truth since it is the only means of acceding to the truth.

All of this has great educative value. To become aware of one's existence vis-à-vis the external world and others represents not only an approach to truth but also a truth in itself. Truth can be not only dialogue and self-knowledge, but also recognition of and communication with others. It is not a question of a dialectic between my truth and someone else's; it is more a matter of a dialogue, an exchange. Interiority will become more pronounced as our reflective grasp of the truth deepens, although it should never become totally cut off from the external world. Who is not truly a being-in-the-world is nothing. Truth is a delicate balance between total identity with exteriority and total isolation in interiority. Our very freedom is defined by this dialogue between interiority and exteriority.

The first step in the search for truth is therefore an awareness of this dualism and the certitude of being able to question oneself as well as what is external to the self. Étienne Borne writes: "I may be mistaken in believing I know who I am; but I cannot be mistaken when I realize that I must be in perpetual quest of my being and engage in constant self-criticism." The first truth we should inculcate in those who have attained a degree of maturity is that they must question themselves. To question oneself is to discover two opposing poles: one, the possibility of affirmation; the other, the possibility of negation. When we discover a truth we also discover that we can negate it. This was one of the important points we made in our first chapter.

Indeed, we may summarize the foregoing by saying that our first insight into the truth is a discovery of the notions of *subject* and *object:* the object being the external world with its evidence and contradictions. The questioning of self also gives rise to that reflective mode of thought that leads to a double consciousness and enables me to regard *myself* as an object, or, as Sartre would say, a "quasi-object."

In the end, we discover in ourselves a contradiction: a possible *yes* and a possible *no.* The discovery of this contradiction is the discovery of our finitude and our freedom. And this, too, is a truth.

TRUTH AND ITS MYSTERY

In the preceding paragraphs we have tried to show two things: that the unity of truth does not exclude a plurality of approaches on the one hand and on the other that the journey toward truth is a perpetual exchange between self and the world and a perpetual self-questioning.

We now wish to show that absolute truth does not exclude the acceptance of mystery or the practice of charity.

The truth *is;* even the skeptic affirms the truth of his being by doubting. It is one thing to know abstractly that there is truth; another to be personally convinced of this. When Christ appeared before Pilate, the skeptic, and said that he had come to bear witness to the truth, Pilate did not ask: "What truth?" but "What is truth?" (John 18:38) Exegetes might wrangle over the translation of this text, but it is clear that in the version most faithful to the Greek, Pilate's question is not about truth but about whether or not there is any truth. To admit that there is truth, without yet knowing what it is, is already to enter upon the quest for truth.

It is also to admit that although affirming its existence we cannot know it totally. To accept the truth is at the same time to recognize its dimension of mystery. This does not mean that the truth as such is mysterious; only that we are unable to see it fully. This is what Urs von Balthasar means when he says that the truth is transcendent, that its mystery is immanent and testifies to our human limitations. To recognize it would lead us into error, if not outright lying and bad faith. The discovery of mystery through knowledge does not impoverish the latter but extends it beyond the accessible. Von Balthasar says: 'We have seen in effect that the truth is not something already made which one has only to possess; rather it is the fruit of a procreation in which the subject participates by his gift of love. In this sense, we create and condition the truth." A question that was widely discussed when I was a student was the following: Is love a form of knowledge? It would perhaps be better to reverse the proposition and say that knowledge is a form of love. The possession of truth always implies love and this is the mystery of truth. We not only receive the truth; we must contribute to it. Truth, while remaining what it is, is never exactly the same thing after knowledge of it has become widespread.

Here a second aspect of the mystery of truth appears: the influence truth undergoes when it becomes known. Truth must be transmitted if it is to remain alive; communication constitutes the tradition that supports it. As von Balthasar writes: "Truth is less the tranquil possession of a certain object than a principle, an instrument of thought, a ferment that enables us to realize progressively the truth in the world and in the community through a process that is never completed. The certitude of truth is a gift that must be distributed immediately to the kingdom of uncertainty where the light of the truth has not yet penetrated." Truth like a seed must be sown without concern whether it will germinate or not. Truth is a commitment, von Balthasar goes on, "but this commitment can only be *action*. Through his life, his activity, and indeed his suffering man must give proof that he is ready to dedicate himself totally to the truth he advances."[8]

Truth is both immutable and in a state of becoming. If we share in the becoming of truth and if the fullness of our being depends on the way in which we transmit it then there can be no place for lying, which would be a diminution of our being.

Whatever our level of education, we are all mediators of the truth. To teach the child that he has a role to play in the affirmation and transmission of the truth will contribute to reducing the climates of bad faith and our propensity for lying.

Truth never overwhelms us. On the contrary, only through it can we define our personality and our individuality. This is no gratuitous affirmation: We can develop our personality only by serving the truth and

8 Von Balthasar, *op. cit.*, p. 164.

bearing witness to it. To take refuge in lying and insincerity is to set up barriers against our human development. It may be a temporary but never a final solution. Each can in his own individual manner possess and express the truth and thus mark it with the seal of his own personality. When truth is thus appropriated we can never communicate it without at the same time communicating something of ourselves. In a double movement we participate in the brilliance of truth's light and in the mystery of something that transcends us.

My being is not merely the fact of existing but the way I understand, assimilate, and spread the truth. This is my way of *being in the world*. To teach the truth is not to impose a system of ready-made references; it is rather to help another fashion his personhood on the basis of the true. Truth does not stifle the self but rather affirms it. To give the truth to another is not merely to give him something external and thus increase what he *has*. It does much more: It increases what he *is*. It is to help him discover his own truth by means of the truth that we offer him. What is therapy other than a way of helping a patient become aware of his own truth?

From the preceding we may draw the following conclusion: There is no private truth. There is one's own truth, which we communicate to others and which others communicate to us. Truth is communion, participation, and dialogue. It is *love*.

TRUTH AND LOVE

We began this chapter with a quotation from Pascal urging us to love the truth, and we are now led to consider the truth as an expression of love.

Truth hidden under a bushel is of interest to no one except a few old narcissistic collectors. I am thinking of those pathetic creatures who own rare paintings or jewelry that they enjoy in solitude. All beauty and value would be lost for them if the enjoyment were shared.

Truth is love. We can communicate with another only through dialogue in which we give and receive. There is no perfect love without reciprocity. But love supposes respect, a respect that is essentially for the mystery of the other. A love predicated upon total possession of the other is merely a love of enslavement between a sadistic subject and a masochistic object. To love is to agree that the other not reveal everything, that he not let himself be entirely possessed. Why? Because in possessing everything we no longer possess anything but an image, a shell devoid of substance. The same holds for the truth. To love the truth is to accept its mystery, however passionate may be our love for it. Perhaps the greatest truth of all is the knowledge that we cannot possess it totally. Otherwise, the truth could be equated with our capacities; it would be under our control. Truth is something that transcends me that I must love precisely because it transcends me. To love the truth is to love it as it is, in the measure that I can attain it. Would our love of a woman whom we understood in the hidden depths of her being be a perfect love? All love supposes respect for the intimacy of the other. The other must be loved without alienating part of his being. He would no longer be lovable if he became identified with the beloved. No one is desirable unless he is fully himself. The loved one's being is augmented by the fact that he is loved. But if he were totally revealed, totally possessed by the lover, his being would become diluted, liquefied, and without interest. The same holds for the truth. We can love it sincerely and approach it authentically only to the extent that we respect its transcendence and realize that we can never totally possess it. To expect to possess it totally would condemn us to a Sisyphian effort of ever beginning again. To think we do totally possess it would merit us the punishment of Prometheus for trying to rival the gods.

The analogy between man's search for the truth and human love yields further parallels. Lovers desire to give as much or even more than they receive. The same thing obtains in the case of our love for the truth. Our search for truth must be a hunger that is never satisfied. This means that we must adopt an attitude that requires love. This attitude is not pure passivity, as though it were merely a question of receiving what others choose to give us; nor is it aggressive as though we greedily wanted to know and possess everything. Our attitude toward the truth ought to be oblative. We must contribute something to it. Our possession of the truth supposes a duty to communicate and share it. Moreover, we must adopt an attitude of disponibility toward it and prepare ourselves for its reception. Perhaps at the moment we least expect it, it will knock at the door. The truth sometimes manifests itself dramatically; most of the time, however, it passes silently like a summer breeze. We must be on the alert to detect it. There are many symbolic indications of this in Scripture: the wise and foolish virgins, the miraculous catch, and so forth. He who does not cast his net catches nothing. Truth comes to those who are ready to receive it as love comes to those who are capable of loving. At this point we begin to understand that truth implies freedom.

TRUTH AND FREEDOM

Our study has enabled us to sketch an approach to
the truth through many apparent contradictions. Love
of the truth? But does truth in the highest sense demand love or submission? The plurality of ways that
lead to the truth? But isn't truth essentially an unfolding? To say now that truth is freedom would seem to
introduce yet another contradiction. Isn't the truth
beyond and outside of our willpower, of what we can
affirm? If truth compels us by the light of evidence in
what sense can we speak of freedom? Yet truth is
essentially freedom. It is because it is love, because its
mystery permits it to be received or refused, that it is
also freedom. De Waelhens, in an examination of the
relationship between freedom and truth, does not hesitate to affirm: "We must recognize, however shocking
it may at first seem, that *the essence of truth is freedom.*"[9] Contrasting man and animals, he demonstrates
that for an animal there is a *given* but no *truth* because
to recognize truth means that we can question it. Interrogation supposes that a negative response is possible.
Animals cannot detach themselves from the given
while man can always question what is given, either in
whole or in part.

Thus from an educational point of view our apprenticeship to truth is parallel to our apprenticeship to
freedom.

It might be objected that mathematical truth ($2 +
2 = 4$) and historical truth (the Bastille fell on July 14,
1789) do not engage our freedom. Here we must distinguish: When mathematical truth is not merely an

[9] De Waelhens, *Phénoménologie et vérité*, P.U.F., 1953.

abstraction and historical truth takes on subjective meaning it seems that our freedom of interpretation, however minimally, is engaged.

We thus see that education must avoid two dangers. Inculcating so much freedom that the student will be in danger of falling into skepticism or subjectivism on the one hand and on the other presenting the truth so rigidly that it stifles the student's personality. Here we must stress both the character of one who receives the truth and one who teaches it. This gives rise to a beneficial and indispensable dialectical play between the intentionality of the teacher and the intentionality of one who receives it. Let us warn once again, however, that truth is not a synthesis of a thesis and antithesis. Let us take an example: The life of an organism is not a compromise between what it is and what nourishes it. It is incorporation, assimilation. Likewise, the truth becomes living when we appropriate it or, more exactly, when we freely choose to accept it. Kierkegaard said that he knows no truth until it becomes living in him. Could a truth no one received still be called a truth?

Truth, freedom, and life are, if not synonyms, at least realities that are so intimately related that to suppress one would amount to suppressing the other. De Waelhens insists on this indissoluble unity and for this reason concludes that the essence of freedom is truth and the essence of the truth is freedom.

Truth and freedom together represent for man that *presence in the world* that enables him to be receptive, if he chooses, to a world of which he is a part but never identical with.

Permanence and transcendence of the truth, historicity of the truth, man's participation in the truth that is both outside of him and within him, his freedom before the truth that he may accept or reject, the freedom to deny and betray it by lying, bad faith, and infidelity—all of this forms the necessary basis of any metaphysics, because we exist only in terms of our relationship to the true.

CONCLUSION

Bearing Witness to the Truth

The intelligent man does not seek to impose on another a truth that is ready-made like a thing; rather he puts himself in the service of a truth that is a life.—JEAN LACROIX

WE HAVE SEEN that the term *lying* means the transmission of a countertruth with the intention to deceive. What should we call the opposite, the transmission of truth? Is it teaching? Education?

Let us repeat what we have already said concerning lying: The liar knows the truth but deforms and dissimulates it. There is no lie if there is no deep conviction that what we say is contrary to what we know and think.

Let us apply this to the transmission of the truth to another. We must absolutely teach what is in conformity with what we think is the truth. In other words we must be as certain as possible that we ourselves possess the truth we wish to transmit. We never possess more than a relative certitude of course; but this is sufficient to enable us to communicate it. We must, therefore, feel ourselves to be in the truth, or at least on the way to truth, to earn the right to transmit it as it is. We would not be educating if we sought shelter

behind such phrases as "I was told" or "It seems that."
To educate is to affirm that what is transmitted corresponds to a truth we believe in. We have seen that truth
is part of being. To transmit the truth is thus to communicate something of oneself. In this way education
becomes *a witness* and not merely the transfer of a
truth-object. J. P. Bagot[1] has some brilliant lines on
this subject. "The teacher does not teach the truth, he
bears witness to it. . . . The attitude with which the
educator should bear witness to the truth consists of a
double relationship: that which binds him to his material and that which binds him to those he teaches." The
teacher is a mediator between the truth and another
and this is at bottom a priestly task. The teacher receives the Word and then transmits it. But this transmission can take place only if there is an exchange, a
dialogue.

A teacher who does not engage in dialogue no longer
teaches. He is no better than a book. Marcel Proust
remembered his philosophy professor, M. Darlu, in
these words: "This great man whose inspired words are
more certain to endure than a book-engendered
thought in me as in so many others." (Preface to
Plaisirs et des jours.) The Proust scholar Jacques
Nathan tells us that M. Darlu's class was in the form
of a dialogue. The program perhaps suffered but not
education in the deepest sense. It is sometimes objected
that in teaching, the material conditions do not favor
dialogue. This may be. But it does not change the fact
that the teacher who never talks with his students will
not be a good teacher; he will have great difficulty
communicating the truth. That is why I have such fond
memories of those mornings in the hospital when I was

[1] J. P. Bagot, in *Cahiers d'éducateurs*, 4 Éditions Fleurus, 1964.

a medical student. The professor, his assistants and students were in constant dialogue. To teach the truth is to seek it together with our students. "My students taught me more than I ever taught them," said one of my teachers. Dialogue leads to depth and is a means of correcting errors that might have otherwise gone unnoticed. The teacher himself often contributes more than he is aware of. Why? Because the truth he bears is greater than he is, although it is always enriched by his personal witness.

The truths I have received are personalized truths; a face is inscribed on each one. I cannot think of Ovid without remembering the country priest who taught me the rudiments of Latin. When I open Racine I remember my secondary school teacher. Lung diseases were taught by an intern who has since become a well-known professor. In psychoanalysis I had a teacher with a blond beard. I remember less the pages of a book than the words of those who taught me.

To teach the truth is to bear witness while receiving the witness of others. In this way we find freedom. Witness is much more important in education than in instruction. The formation of the personality depends essentially upon witness received and given. How would someone act who only learned what he knows from a book? If he has not seen others thinking and acting in a certain way, he will learn little from a book. Witness to the truth implies the dynamism of example.

We might ask whether or not a constant dialogue would risk cutting the truth from all reference to stable principles and whether or not personalized truth would be no more than a private truth. To each his truth!

We touch here upon the double danger mentioned earlier of skepticism and relativism on the one hand

and on the other rigid dogmatism. Bagot deals with this question at some length. First of all, he establishes the two following propositions:

1. Moral truths or principles are not immediately evident or persuasive. They do not automatically move the will.

2. Moral truths are never universally applicable, independent of the psychological makeup of those who receive them.

For these reasons we cannot profess the truth as a professor might give a formal lecture. Rather one "professes" the truth in the strongest sense of the word: that is, a public affirmation of what one believes. If teaching is restricted to imparting principles, then witness is likely to be excluded. Bagot declares that it is impossible to teach morality in an abstract way. "Principles" are no more than the means to moral awareness. They cannot take its place. They draw their worth from the strength of the freedom of those who use them. Bagot distinguishes as does Kierkegaard between *truth as a way* and *truth as a result*. He writes: "If moral truths were on the order of truth as a result, transmissible by simple instruction, they would prevent man from acceding to authentic morality. Indeed they would alienate him from it and burden him under the weight of foreign imperatives; they would restrict his freedom by leading him into that spiritual slavery to the law that St. Paul so frequently denounced. Even though favoring a conformity that is beneficial to the social order, they would spell the end of authentic morality. We would end with the paradox that moral truths killed the truth of morality."

Here we see once more how closely freedom is bound up with truth. To live is to subject truth to a constant dialogue and thus endanger it. Our duty is not only to receive the truth; we must spread it and make it fructify. This is the profound meaning of the parable of the talents. Truth is an adventure we embark upon without duplicity or bad faith and without too much concern about how far we will go. What is important is not the result but the way. To be on the way to truth is already to be in the truth. Moses never knew the Promised Land, but he led his people safely there.